The authors attempt to arrive at an under-
standing of the man who contributed so much
to science and to the concept of man and his
destiny, whose work caused a great revolution in the world's thinking.

CHARLES DARWIN

and his world

CHARLES DARWIN

and his world

BY JULIAN HUXLEY
AND H. B. D. KETTLEWELL

A STUDIO BOOK

THE VIKING PRESS · NEW YORK

Shrewsbury from Coton Hill: an early-nineteenth-century engraving

INTRODUCTION

'I was also troubled with palpitations and pain about the heart and like many a young ignorant man, especially one with a smattering of medical knowledge, was convinced that I had heart disease. I did not consult any Doctor, as I fully expected to hear the verdict that I was not fit for a voyage and I was resolved to go at all hazards.' Forty-five years later Charles Darwin recorded this vivid memory of the past. It was the autumn of 1831 and he was then aged twenty-two. For two months he had been kicking his heels at Plymouth awaiting the departure of the *Beagle* on its voyage round the world. He was in conflict within himself as to the wisdom of his decision to accompany her as naturalist. He wrote in the little notebook which he always kept: 'These months very miserable.' Yet this was probably the most important moment of his life. For the next five years the voyage of the *Beagle* was to change not only his own attitude to life, his beliefs and basic concepts, but it was to provide food for thought for millions of people, it was to produce schisms in the Church and a century of argument among scientists. It was also to lay the most important foundation-stone for a fuller understanding of living things and the world we live in.

It is therefore essential to study the man as he was before so great an event in his life and to compare him with the man we find afterwards. Thanks to the notebooks and journal he kept so meticulously during the voyage we have also a great advantage in being able to examine, almost daily, how new impacts and new experiences moulded his rapidly changing views.

Every individual is the product of two, and only two, factors: firstly the characters he inherits from his parents (be they emotions, physique, or powers of reasoning) and secondly the effects on these of outside influences which he experiences during his lifetime. The life of Charles Darwin, because it was divided clearly into three distinct phases, and because each of these is well documented, gives the biographer ideal opportunities for analysing his metamorphosis. He himself in his autobiography later admitted, 'The voyage of the *Beagle* has been by far the most important event in my life and has determined my whole career.'

Was Darwin primarily a hypochondriac at the age of twenty-two, as the opening quotation suggests, or were the recurring periods of ill-health, lassitude, and headaches so constantly referred to in his letters during the third and longest phase of his life due to the sequelae of Chagas' disease which he may have contracted in South America during the voyage of the *Beagle*? How much did his great mistake in 1839 (over the parallel roads of Glen Roy, which he erroneously concluded had been once at sea-level) delay the publication of his great idea? Why did the period of gestation of this thorough and painstaking man last more than twenty years before the delivery of his pronouncements, when the brain-child was ready to be born, fully developed, at a much earlier date? Why was the injection by Wallace necessary to bring about parturition?

Only by studying Charles Darwin in the three phases of his life can we come to understand the man who contributed so much to science, to religious and philosophical discussion, and to the concepts of Man and his destiny. These have affected in so many ways the lives of every human being who has lived since. One wonders, for instance, how much the ideologies of Karl Marx, who was living in obscurity in London at the height of the evolutionary furore, were affected by the theories of Charles Darwin and their implications. The Church, after a hasty retreat, has had to become more tolerant, and Man for the first time has been able to discover his place and role in Nature.

The Mount House, Shrewsbury: Darwin's birthplace

THE PRELUDE (1809–1831)

'When I left the school I was for my age neither high nor low in it; and I believe that I was considered by all my masters and by my father as a very ordinary boy, rather below the common standard in intellect.' (*Autobiography*, 1887)

CHARLES DARWIN was born on 12 February 1809 in Shrewsbury, where his father Robert had a successful medical practice. Robert Waring Darwin was a formidable man, over six feet tall and weighing twenty-four stone. Charles states, 'he was the largest man whom I ever saw'. He had remarkable powers of perception of his patients' ills and these he discussed freely with his son, anticipating his eventual entry into the medical profession (although he himself loathed it: 'Every road out of Shrewsbury is associated in my mind with some painful event'). Charles in his early years worshipped his father, 'the kindest man I ever knew', yet at the same time he was severely inhibited by him.

Erasmus Darwin (*right*) and his second son

Charles's grandfather was Erasmus Darwin, FRS, who died in 1802. He left to posterity two books recording his scientific views in verse—*The Botanic Garden* and *Zoonomia*. His son Robert (Charles's father) did not relish these, nor had he been on particularly good terms with his father. Paternal conflict is clearly seen in three generations of Darwins.

Charles's mother, who was a daughter of Josiah Wedgwood, FRS, died when he was eight, and her death affected him profoundly, though he admitted later, 'It is odd that I can remember hardly anything about her except her death-bed, her black velvet gown and her curiously constructed work-table.' Charles had one younger and three older sisters, and his only brother, Erasmus, was five years his senior. They were a closely knit family, and up to the age of eight his education was carried out at home by his sister Caroline, who was nine years his senior. She found him somewhat slow.

Schooldays   He then became a day-boy at the school of the Reverend G. Case, a Unitarian minister, where he stayed about a year. Already at this date he showed a passion for natural history by collecting 'all sorts of things, shells, seals, franks, coins and minerals'. As he remarks later, 'The passion for collecting . . . was clearly innate, as none of my sisters or brother ever had the taste.'

Dr Robert Waring Darwin,
Charles's father

Susannah Darwin, Charles's mother

Charles, aged six, and his
youngest sister Catherine

At the age of nine he entered Dr Butler's school at Shrewsbury, where he remained for the next seven years. Though he was a boarder his home was less than a mile away and he recalls in his autobiography that he often ran there 'before locking up at night'. He also observes how advantageous this was to him 'by keeping up home affections and interests'. Retrospectively Darwin was critical of his school. 'Nothing could have been worse for the development of my mind than Dr Butler's school, as it was strictly classical, nothing else being taught except a little ancient geography and history.' As a means of education, school to him 'was simply a blank'. However, during his schooldays Charles read extensively in his spare time. In particular he delighted in poetry (Byron and Shakespeare) though later in life this ceased to give him pleasure. *Wonders of the World* filled him with a desire to travel, 'ultimately fulfilled by the voyage of the *Beagle*'. Gilbert White's *Selborne* made a great impression on him and was instrumental in arousing his interest in bird-watching. 'In my simplicity I remember wondering why every gentleman did not become an ornithologist.' But it was other influences outside Dr Butler's school which contributed so much to his earliest interest in science: the demonstration by his uncle (father of Francis Galton) of how a barometer worked, his brother's keenness on chemistry which led to their doing experiments in a makeshift laboratory in the toolshed (an activity which was frowned on by Dr Butler and incidentally earned

The fly-leaf of Darwin's school atlas: schoolboys have changed little in a century and a half

The Old Schools, Shrewsbury: engraving, *c.* 1820

Charles the nickname of 'Gas'). Still earlier, at the age of ten, during a holiday on the Welsh coast with one of his sisters, he became engrossed in insects (chiefly butterflies and moths), many of which he noted were not to be found in Shropshire.

His health during his schooldays seems to have been excellent, except for a bout of scarlet fever at the age of nine, and he was proud of his prowess as a runner.

With this somewhat inconspicuous school career behind him, Charles left school at sixteen and entered the University of Edinburgh, where he spent the next two years. He left, in fact, because his father decided 'he was doing no good at school'.

Academically he had got nowhere; he rebelled against the type of education he had had; science was not recognized as being within the realm of a gentleman's occupation. Emotionally he was normal, though he admits to beating a puppy when a very little boy 'for enjoying the sense of power'. He also admits to inventing stories in order to attract attention. An interesting example of this is that he told another boy that he 'could produce various coloured poly-anthuses . . . by watering them with certain coloured fluids'. Later he states that he 'had many friends among the schoolboys, whom I loved dearly, and I think that my disposition was then very affectionate'. These admissions are now recognized as being perfectly normal in the metamorphosis of youth, but not so in 1876. They certainly bear witness to his complete honesty.

At an early age Charles had experienced a wealth of illness in others. His mother was a chronic invalid; his brother Erasmus suffered constant ill-health. Finally, on his father's insistence, Charles began 'attending some of the poor people, chiefly children and women, in Shrewsbury' during the summer holidays, after leaving Dr Butler's school and before entering Edinburgh University. There is also considerable evidence that because of his failure at school Charles was by this time developing a guilt-complex towards his father: surely the ideal background for future psychoneuroses! Nor would his inheritance buffer him against these. His paternal grandfather, Erasmus Darwin, suffered from a bad stammer, as did his Uncle Charles. His Uncle Erasmus committed suicide at the age of forty. A tendency to neurosis can also be traced on his mother's side. Her father is believed to have had nervous breakdowns, and her brother, Tom Wedgwood, had fits of depression with 'marked abdominal distress'. With such a background it is surprising that Charles became the normal healthy schoolboy that he was.

Edinburgh University

When Charles was sixteen his father decided that medicine was to be his son's calling. This decision seems to have coincided with Charles's realization that 'father would leave me property enough to subsist on with some comfort'. With these thoughts and the recent memories of his summer holidays attending the sick poor in the slums of Shrewsbury, Charles arrived at Edinburgh University in the autumn of 1825. He was accompanied by his brother Erasmus, who was completing his medical course, also with some misgivings. Not surprisingly, Charles found the prospects grim. In fact, the Edinburgh medical course was anathema. 'Dr Duncan's lectures on Materia Medica at eight o'clock on a winter's morning are something awful to remember.' 'Dr Munro made his lectures on human anatomy dull.' 'I saw two very bad operations . . . but I ran away before they were completed.' Above all, he resented the lack of opportunity of gaining experience in dissection. He must at an early stage have decided that the call of the medical profession was not for him.

His medical course at Edinburgh must be looked upon as a complete failure, though Edinburgh itself, during his two years there, provided opportunities in other directions. This was the age of small societies where undergraduates met and read papers: the Wernerian Society, where Darwin was occasionally taken by Dr Grant, the only man at Edinburgh who had a word to say for evolution

Erasmus Alvey Darwin,
Charles's elder brother

(though with a Lamarckian outlook); the Plinian Society, where Darwin gave
his first paper 'On the ova of *Flustra*'; the Royal Medical Society, which he
'attended pretty regularly but as the subjects were exclusively medical I did not
care about them'. Nevertheless, besides Dr Grant he met several stimulating
characters: the American naturalist Audubon, the geologist W. F. Ainsworth,
'who knew a little about many subjects' and was 'very glib with the tongue',
and kind-hearted Dr Coldstream, who contributed 'good zoological articles',
with whom he 'examined marine animals on the shore of the Firth of Forth',
and who was responsible for Darwin's interest in a Bryozoan like *Flustra*. It is
probably more important that a Negro who had worked with Charles Waterton
gave him 'lessons for payment' on stuffing birds and animals.

Christ's College, Cambridge:
the Gateway

He attended lectures on geology by Robert Jameson, Professor of Natural History, which 'were incredibly dull' and made him determined 'never as long as I live to read a book on geology'. By contrast, at home in the holidays Mr Cotton, the local Shrewsbury geologist, fired his enthusiasm with local rocks. It was indeed a strange curriculum for a medico!

Only after Charles had been at Edinburgh for two years did his father learn from his daughters that his son did not wish to become a physician. Charles would not face telling Father himself. Brother Erasmus had already given up the idea of practising medicine; Father, at the age of sixty-one, nearing the end of his medical career, wanted to hand over his practice. Small wonder that Darwin spent more and more time outside Shrewsbury at Maer with his Uncle Josiah (Jos) Wedgwood; 'life there was perfectly free'. There is no doubt that Darwin made every effort to avoid holidays at home at this stage of his life. He toured Scotland (Dundee and Stirling), Ireland (Belfast and Dublin), and finally London, and made his only continental visit, to Paris, all with Uncle Jos.

Meanwhile, Father had decided that his son must become a clergyman, as 'he was very properly vehement against my turning into an idle sporting man'. A degree at Cambridge was therefore necessary. At the age of nineteen Charles again had to undertake a complete reorientation of his life. Dr Duncan's Materia Medica was replaced by Paley's *Evidences of Christianity*, 'and as I did not then in the least doubt the strict and literal truth of every word of the Bible, I soon persuaded myself that our Creed must be fully accepted'.

But once again in his own estimation he was a failure, and later he writes, 'During the three years which I spent at Cambridge my time there was wasted as far as the academic studies were concerned as completely as at Edinburgh and at school.' His passion for shooting got him into a sporting set 'including some dissipated low-minded young men. . . . I know that I ought to feel ashamed of days and evenings thus spent.' His guilt-complex was now complete—by his own admission he was a failure.

Nevertheless, 'by answering well the examination questions in Paley, by doing Euclid well and by not failing miserably in Classics' he gained a good pass degree. As at Edinburgh, any benefits he derived at Cambridge were achieved through his personal friendships with senior members of the University staff. Once again, most of his friends were geologists and botanists, but a few

G Staircase, Front Court: Darwin's rooms at Christ's College were on the first floor, above the doorway

Adam Sedgwick, FRS,
Professor of Geology

were the result of his other interests, his love of music and good paintings. Two men in particular left their indelible stamp on him, firstly J. S. Henslow, the Professor of Botany, and secondly Adam Sedgwick, the Professor of Geology.

Henslow, who was only thirteen years Darwin's senior, appears to have taken him immediately into the bosom of his family and was later responsible for his obtaining the post of unpaid naturalist on the *Beagle*. Henslow, a deeply religious man, was a scientist with a wide knowledge of 'botany, entomology, chemistry, mineralogy and zoology'. His concept of University training in science was years in advance of the time: he took his botany students on 'field excursions on foot or in coaches to distant places', and he 'kept open house once every week where undergraduates . . . used to meet in the evening'. Darwin was privileged to take 'long walks with him on most days'. Never has opportunity provided a more apt teacher or a more receptive pupil. Darwin revered him and imbibed this great man's thoughts and views.

But Darwin, who we must not forget was reading for Holy Orders, by his own efforts established friendships with many others: Albert Way, sub-sequently a well-known ornithologist, and H. Thompson, later an M.P. and leading agriculturist (both of whom were passionate collectors of beetles); Dr William Whewell, Master of Trinity College; Mr Dawes, afterwards Dean of Hereford. It may well be asked how it was that an undergraduate of so little

The Rev. John Stevens Henslow,
Professor of Botany

distinction could command these personal friendships. Darwin's own views on this were enlightening. 'Looking back, I infer there must have been something in me a little superior to the common run of youth, otherwise the above-mentioned men, so much older than me and higher in academic position, would never have allowed me to associate with them.'

Darwin left Cambridge in the spring of 1831. His friend Henslow, the botanist, at whose home he had latterly been living, had persuaded him to become interested in geology. He also arranged for Darwin to join Professor Sedgwick on a geological excursion to North Wales. Henslow had taught him the importance of 'long-continued minute observations'. Sedgwick now showed him 'that Science consists in grouping facts so that general laws or conclusions may be drawn from them'. It was these two men more than any others who were to influence his future. Cambridge was certainly not in vain.

About this time Darwin read Humboldt's *Personal Narrative*, which immediately gave him the urge to visit Tenerife. He planned a trip, made enquiries about ships, and laboriously began to learn Spanish. The time was indeed ripe for some such expedition. Henslow saw this and, religious man that he was, must certainly have realized that Darwin's heart was not in the Church, nor would his personality be satisfied by becoming a country parson. He must also by now have had indications of Darwin's scientific potential.

Josiah Wedgwood II—
'Uncle Jos'

FitzRoy's offer   On 24 August 1831, Henslow wrote to Darwin telling him of the offer by Captain Robert FitzRoy 'to give up part of his own cabin to any young man who would volunteer to go with him without pay as a naturalist to the voyage of the *Beagle*. . . . I have stated that I consider you to be the best qualified person I know of who is likely to undertake such a situation. I state this not in the supposition of your being a *finished* naturalist, but as amply qualified for collect⁄ing, observing and noting, anything worthy to be noted in Natural History. . . . Don't put on any modest doubts or fears about your qualifications, for I assure you I think you are the very man they are in search of.'

Darwin was delighted, but his father objected strongly; once again his plans for his son's future were being circumvented. 'So I wrote that evening and refused the offer.' He must indeed have felt frustrated. He left home next morning, 1 September, for the opening day of partridge shooting with Uncle Jos at Maer. A list of his father's objections was drawn up by Charles. Josiah Wedgwood answered them and set out the next day for Shrewsbury to present Charles's case in person. This was probably the first time the inflexible will of his father was overcome. His son's wishes were granted and he 'took leave' of his home on 2 October. The *Beagle* finally set sail on 27 December with a still somewhat hesitant Charles Darwin aboard.

The New Victualling Office, Devil's Point, Devonport. From the near-by dockyard the *Beagle* sailed on her famous voyage. (*See map on page 129*)

THE EXPERIENCE:

THE VOYAGE OF THE *BEAGLE* (1831–1836)

'My second life will then commence and it shall be as a birthday for the rest of my life.' (Letter to Captain FitzRoy, 17 October 1831)

CHARLES DARWIN, BA (Cantab.) in Theology, Euclid, and the Classics, left England as naturalist to the *Beagle* with no scientific degrees whatsoever. On the other hand he had what was even more important, a wealth of practical experience in the field under the guidance of two exceptional men, Stevens Henslow and Adam Sedgwick. He had learned how to stuff birds and he had already made collections of fossils, rocks and beetles (which were looked after in his absence by Henslow). Furthermore, he was what his Uncle Jos called 'a man of enlarged curiosity'. His presence on the *Beagle* was made possible by his having his own private means, as also had been his time at Edinburgh and

HMS *Beagle*: side elevation,
1 Darwin's seat in the
Captain's cabin;
2 Darwin's seat in the
poop cabin;
3 drawers for specimens;
4 azimuth compass

Captain Robert FitzRoy:
portrait painted after his
promotion to Vice-Admiral

Cambridge. It is doubtful if under today's system of competitive examinations Darwin would have gained entry to either University. How many other Darwins and 'men of enlarged curiosity' do we pass over today? How long shall we take to realize that it is curiosity, initiative, originality, and the ruthless application of honesty that count in research—much more than feats of logic or memory alone?

For the next five years Darwin was to travel the world, cut off from civilization except for occasional letters from home. He was influenced by what he saw, by the few books he had room for in his cabin, and by the personnel on the *Beagle*. Scientifically he was on his own.

While awaiting the day of sailing at Devonport he had drawn up a programme for daily routine. 'It is difficult to mark out any plan and without method on shipboard I am sure little will be done. The principal objects are 1st: collecting, observing and reading in all branches of Natural History that I possibly can manage. Observations in Meteorology, French and Spanish, Mathematics and a little Classics, perhaps not more than the Greek Testament on Sundays.' What strange bedfellows, but how fully was the first intention consummated! How strange the idea of Classics, Mathematics and the Greek Testament—or was this a subconscious urge to satisfy his father's wishes?

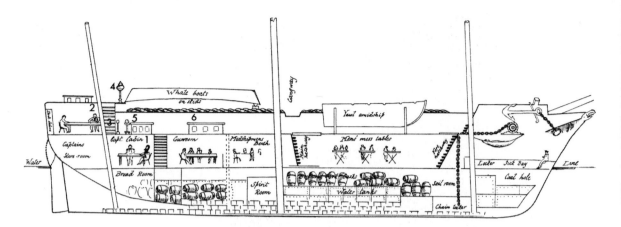

There was not a great deal of space for books on the *Beagle*, but we know some of the literature he took: Humboldt's *Personal Narrative*, which was inscribed 'J. S. Henslow, to his friend C. Darwin on his departure from England upon a voyage round the world. 21st September 1831'; and Milton's *Paradise Lost*, which accompanied him on all his excursions inland.

One of the great disadvantages of a sailing ship like the *Beagle* was that the limited number of individuals aboard had to live in close contact for long periods. Foremost among the personnel was the Captain, Robert FitzRoy, four years Darwin's senior; an aristocrat, and an illegitimate descendant of Charles II, FitzRoy was a devout Christian and a dynamic personality. Writing home in 1832 with his earliest views of the voyage, Darwin states, 'I should not call him a clever man, yet I feel convinced nothing is too great or too high for him. His ascendancy over every body is quite curious . . . altogether he is the strongest marked character I ever fell in with.'

Captain FitzRoy

Yet he was a most difficult shipmate—especially as Captain. 'FitzRoy's temper was a most unfortunate one and was shown not only by passion, but by fits of long-continued moroseness against those who had offended him. His temper was usually worst in the early morning and with his eagle eye he could usually detect something amiss about the ship and was then unsparing in his blame.' 'He was also somewhat suspicious and occasionally in very low spirits, on one occasion bordering on insanity. . . . The difficulty of living on good terms with a captain of a man-of-war is much increased by its being almost mutinous to answer him as one would answer anyone else.' Darwin had several quarrels with him on the *Beagle*, the first early in the voyage at Bahia, when FitzRoy 'defended and praised slavery which I abominated'. So fierce was the argument that Darwin 'thought that I should have been compelled to leave the ship'. In retrospect, how strange the devout Christian FitzRoy

'Am I not a man and a brother?' Wedgwood cameo on the anti-slavery theme

The mole, Palace and Cathedral, Rio de Janeiro

championing slavery, the eventual atheist Darwin rebelling · against an accepted practice.

Shipmates   Other members of the crew whom Darwin got to know well were Philip King, midshipman, and Augustus Earle, draughtsman, who shared lodgings with Darwin whilst the *Beagle* was at Rio de Janeiro; Charles Musters, volunteer, first-class, John Lort Stokes and Bartholomew James Sullivan (both destined to become admirals), and Simms Covington, 'fiddler and boy to Poop Cabin', but who during the second year of the voyage became Darwin's personal attendant at £60 a year by agreement with both his father and FitzRoy.

Darwin taught him to shoot and to stuff birds. On 3 July 1833, he wrote, 'I shall now make a fine collection in birds and quadrupeds which before took up far too much time.' 'During the first two years my old passion for shooting survived in nearly full force, and I shot myself all the birds and animals for my collection, but gradually I gave up my gun more and more and finally all together to my servant, as shooting interfered with my work.' The knowledge which Charles Waterton's Negro in Edinburgh had imparted to Darwin was thus passed on to Covington, without whom Darwin could not have amassed the material he did nor had the time for studying it. Now he had more leisure for thinking and formulating theories.

There were three very strange characters also aboard the *Beagle*, Fuegia Basket, York Minster, and Jemmy Button. It is rather surprising that Darwin does not refer more to these unusual people in his earlier notebooks. These three Fuegians had been taken as hostages in 1829 by Captain FitzRoy on a previous voyage when his whaling boat was stolen by the natives. The Captain, a very religious man, decided to take his wild naked hostages back to Britain and to give them a Christian education. Fuegia and York married there.

During the voyage, it is possible to see the slow metamorphosis of Darwin's scientific views, particularly in geology but also in botany and zoology, and his belief in the value of fossils as evidence of the relation of present-day species with the past. By synthesizing these by the end of the voyage (1836) he was convinced of the significance of geographical grouping and the probability of evolution of one species from another by means of natural selection—it is likely also that he was largely convinced of the origin and evolution of man himself.

The first few weeks of the voyage were marred by sea-sickness. 'I will now give all the dear-bought experience I have gained about sea-sickness. In the first place the misery is excessive and far exceeds what a person would suppose who had never been at sea more than a few days.' The Bay of Biscay and Cape Finisterre were hell: 'wretchedly out of sorts and very sick'. Nevertheless, in spite of this he records seeing porpoises and stormy petrels around the ship, and he spent his time reading 'Humboldt's glowing accounts of tropical scenery'.

On 6 January he saw Tenerife and its famous Peak of Teide. 'It is now about 11 o'clock and I must have another gaze on this long-wished-for object of my ambition.' His original plans with Henslow were being fulfilled. But 'Oh! misery, misery, we were just preparing to drop anchor within half a mile of Santa Cruz when a boat came alongside, bringing with it our death-warrant. The Consul declared we must perform a rigorous quarantine of twelve days.' Once again he was frustrated. He could only gaze on Tenerife from afar.

South of the Canaries Darwin began field work. He devised his own method of collecting plankton. He concocted 'a bag four feet deep, made of bunting and attached to a semicircular bow', which must have been one of the earliest plankton tow-nets. He trolled this behind the ship and collected huge numbers of small creatures: 'many . . . so low in the scale of Nature, are most exquisite in their forms and rich colours. It creates a feeling of wonder that so much beauty should be apparently created for such little purpose.' Within two weeks of leaving England he had commenced to question orthodox beliefs.

On 16 January 1832, Darwin first landed on a tropical shore, the island of St Jago, in the Cape Verde Islands. 'I expected a good deal, for I had read Humboldt's descriptions and I was afraid of disappointments: how utterly vain

From the top: Fuegia Basket, York Minster, and Jemmy Button, as they appeared in London before returning to Tierra del Fuego

Crossing the Line in the *Beagle*

such fear is, none can tell but those who have experienced what I today have. . . . I returned to the shore, treading on volcanic rocks, hearing the notes of unknown birds and seeing new insects fluttering about still newer flowers . . . it has been for me a glorious day, like giving to a blind man eyes, he is overwhelmed with what he sees and cannot easily comprehend it. Such are my feelings and such may they remain.' The enthusiasm, the new approach, and the questioning of orthodox opinion became apparent in the first three weeks of the voyage.

It was in these islands that Darwin at the age of twenty-three first produced the theory that 'the hard white rocks' were brought about by molten lava flowing over the sea-bed and baking the triturated shells and coral. He even thought of writing a book on the geology of the countries he visited. Fifty years later he admits, 'That was a memorable hour to me.'

On 17 February, with the usual ceremonies, Darwin crossed the Equator for the first time: 'The constable blindfolded me and thus led along buckets of water were thundered all around.'

Brazil   He first set foot in South America on 28 February at Bahia. 'The land is a chaos of delight, out of which a world of future and more quiet pleasure will rise. I am at present fitted only to read Humboldt: he like another Sun illuminates everything I behold.'

Bahia: the Church of San Salvador

The impact of Brazil on Darwin was immense. He writes in ecstasy, 'What can be imagined more delightful than to watch Nature in its grandest form in regions of the tropics. . . . Twiners entwining twiners—tresses like hair—beautiful Lepidoptera—silence—hosannah—Frog habits like toad—slow jumpers—'. 'Here he [the naturalist] suffers a pleasant nuisance in not being able to walk one hundred yards without being fairly tied to the spot by some new and wondrous creature.'

It is here also we get vivid glimpses of the man as well as the scientist; his growing capacity for assessing people. He despises the average Brazilian; he praises the Negro slaves. 'It is never pleasant to submit to the insolence of men in office; but to the Brazilians, who are as contemptible in their minds as their persons are miserable, it is nearly intolerable.' Of the slaves he says, 'I hope the day will come when they will assert their own rights and forget to avenge their wrongs.'

Darwin found lodgings at Botofogo with his artist friend Earle, and King, who was midshipman on the *Beagle*. Botofogo in 1832 was a quiet little village outside Rio de Janeiro, situated on a lagoon: today it is a built-up suburban resort. Behind it is the peak of Corcovado, its slopes covered with forests to a height of over 2,000 feet. This was to be his base for the next three months. Within four days of his arrival, Darwin, having moved his 'goods and chattels' to Botofogo, set out on a three-week trek on horseback with five others—surely the perfect method of introduction to a new country. His speed of action at this period of his life contrasts with his later lack of energy. Moreover, he must at this time have been extremely robust. On many occasions he got up before daylight and rode fifteen miles before breakfast, and on this excursion he travelled several hundred miles on horseback to Macae and back. Little did he think that within nine years he would have to admit to his friend Lyell, 'My father scarcely seems to expect that I shall become strong for some years', and to FitzRoy, 'I have nothing to wish for excepting stronger health to go on with the subjects to which I have joyfully determined to devote my life.'

A collector's
routine
When working from base Darwin followed a routine. He collected on alternate days, the intervening days being used for preserving and labelling specimens and for reading. When the opportunity presented itself he dispatched fossils and geological specimens home.

On his return to Rio he spent the next few weeks making collections of marine shells, corallines, plants, spiders, and beetles, the first two from the beach near Botofogo, the last very frequently in the near-by Corcovado forests. 'These days have glided away very pleasantly but with nothing particular to mark their passage.' He was indeed fortunate to refuse a snipe shoot at Macacu: all eight of his *Beagle* friends who went were taken ill with fever and three died, 'including poor little Musters'.

Apart from his intense interest in geology at this time, he daily records new observations in natural history: a vampire bat which he actually witnessed biting a horse's withers; experiments on glow-worms; a swallowtail butterfly which made clicking noises in flight; a Brazilian stinkhorn fungus which attracts the same genera of beetles as does its European congener; the manœuvres of the army ants while foraging.

In his collecting methods he attempted sampling all orders, not specializing in one more than another. 'I may mention, as a common instance of one day's collecting (23 June 1832) when I was not attending particularly to the Coleop-tera, that I caught 68 species of that order.' He writes that 37 species of Arachnida (spiders) which he 'brought home, will be sufficient to prove that I was not paying over-much attention to the generally favoured order of Coleoptera'.

The *Beagle* left Rio on 5 July 1832, and headed south for Montevideo. 'Everything shows we are steering for barbarous regions, all the officers have stowed away their razors and intend allowing their beards to grow in a truly patriarchal fashion.' Darwin now had three weeks to arrange his Brazilian material before the next port of call. Throughout the voyage periods at sea gave Darwin opportunities to think (between his never-ending bouts of sea-sickness) and to organize his collections.

Corcovado Mountain,
Rio de Janeiro

On their arrival at Montevideo a revolution was taking place and the *Beagle*'s personnel were advised not to land (except on Rat Island). 'The revolutions in these countries are quite laughable; some years ago in Buenos Aires they had fourteen revolutions in twelve months.' The treeless green plains reminded him of Cambridgeshire: 'The view . . . is one of the most uninteresting I ever beheld.' The *Beagle*, because of the political upheaval, proceeded on her way up the broad Rio de la Plata to Buenos Aires. On arrival an Argentinian guardship fired on her. This 'insult to the British Flag' was duly dealt with, the Governor sending his apologies. This was Darwin's first introduction to Argentina, where during the next year he was to make two further visits. The *Beagle* then returned to Montevideo where Captain FitzRoy was requested to land in order to protect private property. 'The politicks of the place are quite unintelligible.' Apart from revolutions he also obtained his first experience of many South American animals, such as ostriches (rheas) and llamas (guanacos) in this region.

The Custom House, Montevideo

His health at this time seems to have been excellent. At Montevideo in August 1832 Darwin remarks that when he and two others were out ostrich shooting, 'if the sport was not very good the exercise was most delightful'. His two companions, however, 'found themselves so tired that they declared they could move no further'.

Before returning to Buenos Aires, the *Beagle* went first through gradually worsening weather as far as Bahia Blanca, Patagonia, 'sailing slowly along the coast' in order to survey it—hundreds of miles 'of sandy hillocks without a break or change . . . the most desolate place I have ever visited'. It was at Bahia Blanca that Darwin first saw the native method of hunting ostriches (and other animals), by fouling their legs with the bolas—'two stones covered with leather and united with a thin plaited thong'. He ate roast armadillos and ostrich eggs: of the latter '44 were in two nests'.

On one occasion he was marooned on shore for the night by a gale: 'We breakfasted on some small birds and two gulls and a large Hawk which was found dead on the beach. . . . I never knew how painful cold could be.' It was here that he first found and later described the fossil bones of the giant sloth (*Megatherium*), which 'must have been as large as a rhinoceros': fossil relics of the extinct giant armadillos (*Glyptodonts*) 'seemed to be related to extant species'. Whenever the *Beagle* anchored inshore, as it frequently did 'to take observations', he collected fossils.

The *Beagle* arrived back on 26 October at Montevideo, where mail from England awaited them: 'receiving letters unfits one for any occupation'. Darwin also received by this same post the second volume of Lyell's *Principles of Geology*, the book which was to influence him so much during the rest of the voyage.

The *Beagle*'s second visit to Buenos Aires lasted only eight days. On the day of arrival 'we immediately went out riding: there is no way of enjoying the shore so thoroughly as on horseback'. During his stay Darwin visited the Museum: 'although esteemed as second to none by the inhabitants, it is very poor'. He was delighted with the señoritas; he writes to his sister Caroline (November 1832): 'Our chief amusement was riding about and admiring the Spanish ladies. After watching one of these angels gliding down the street, involuntarily we groaned out, "How foolish English women are, they can neither walk nor dress." I am sorry for you all. It would do the whole tribe of you a great deal of good to come out to Buenos Aires.'

Hunting guanacos with the bolas

Tierra del Fuego   The *Beagle* revictualled at Montevideo and Darwin packed up his geological specimens to be sent direct back to England. They sailed on 26 November for Tierra del Fuego, the tip of South America where they arrived three weeks later —three weeks of 'doldrums' interspersed with storms along a largely uncharted coastline. One of the objects of the expedition was to return the three Fuegians, Jemmy Button, York Minster and his wife Fuegia Basket, now indoctrinated with Christian beliefs, to their native land. They were accompanied by a missionary, the Reverend Richard Matthews. Considerable thought had been given to the project. As well as crop seeds such as cabbage, wheat, and root vegetables, the Missionary Society had donated equipment they considered essential. Darwin remarks, 'The choice of articles showed the most culpable folly and negligence. Wine-glasses, butter-bolts, tea-trays, soup-turins [*sic*], mahogany dressing case, fine white linen, beaver hats and an endless variety of similar things.' The lack of imagination must have indeed irked.

The native Fuegians turned out to be completely untrustworthy: 'I would not have believed how entire the difference between savage and civilized man is . . . their language does not deserve to be called articulate. Captain Cook says it is like a man clearing his throat. . . . I believe if the world was searched, no lower grade of men could be found.' They lived in wigwams, and at a latitude of 55° S. survived all weathers sleeping naked on the ground. Like the extinct

Tierra del Fuego: the Darwin range from the air

Ona Indians from
the interior of
Tierra del Fuego

strandloopers of South Africa they existed largely on shellfish, and hence, as these are soon exhausted, they migrated.

Not until 3 January 1833 was a suitable place for their settlement found. The Fuegians and their missionary were left for three days. 'From the moment of our leaving, a regular system of plunder commenced. Matthews had lost all his things', and decided to leave. Darwin remarks, 'I am afraid whatever other things this excursion to England produces, it will not be conducive to their happiness.' The experiment was a complete failure. Thirty years later Fuegia Basket who, during her visit to England, had been presented to William IV and Queen Adelaide, was found by the missionary Bridges to be a 'miserable old woman', while Jemmy Button had been the instigator of a massacre of 'missionaries and sailors as they prayed in a half-finished church'.

The *Beagle* returned to Buenos Aires in order to spend the southern winter there. *En route*, five weeks were passed on the Falkland Islands. On 24 March 1833, Darwin records: 'We have never before stayed so long at a place with so little for the Journal.' Nevertheless, a few days earlier he states: 'The whole aspect of the Falkland Islands was ever changed to my eyes from that walk, for I found the rock abounding with shells: and these of the most exciting Geological aera.' Also he was able to transfer to one of the smaller subsidiary schooners in order to visit the Rio Negro and Bay of St Joseph. 'For the scholar of geology this is of the highest interest to me . . . the divisions of the strata run for miles together exactly parallel to the surface of the sea . . . it looks an El Dorado to a Geologist . . . they abounded with fossil shells.'

On his return to the Rio de la Plata Darwin took up residence at Maldonado, which was to be his base for the next three weeks. He carried out a 'little excursion' on horseback 'which besides an outline of the geology, has given me a very good opportunity of seeing both the country and its wild Gaucho inhabitants'.

For the next six weeks Darwin made extensive collections from Maldonado. 'My only object is completing the collection of birds and animals. . . . One day's collecting and the next arranging.' Plans were made for 'next summer to double the Horn. . . . My heart exults whenever I think of all my glorious prospects of the future.' His recent collections were packed and dispatched.

With the immediate future settled Darwin now undertook a series of expeditions, the first to survey the Rio Negro, the second from the town of Patagones to his old haunts at Bahia Blanca and back overland to Buenos Aires. 'The death-like stillness of the plain, the dogs keeping watch, the gypsy-group of Gauchos making their beds around the fire, has left in my mind a strongly marked picture of the first night, which will not soon be forgotten.'

At this period of his life Darwin underwent great physical hardships, experiencing the deprivations of thirst which 'rendered me very weak'. He outrode his Gaucho guides 'and as a Gaucho cannot walk I gave up my horse and took to my feet'. He must indeed have been tough and also fearless. Before starting his second expedition from Patagones to Buenos Aires, Darwin spent two weeks collecting fossils at Bahia Blanca. Ancient flint arrow-heads convinced him that the Indians must originally have lived by bow and arrow in the same way as the Fuegians did in 1833. He surmised that the use of the bolas had developed following the introduction of the horse to South America. 'Yet the change of habits, proved by the frequency of the arrow-heads, convinced me that the horse was not an original inhabitant.'

It was during his enforced stay here that Darwin discovered a second species of rhea, later to be named after him *Struthio darwinii* by Gould.

An Argentinian gaucho:
'a Gaucho cannot walk',
Darwin noted in his diary

On 8 September, Darwin and a guide set out for Buenos Aires—400 miles of hard riding. On 16 September he arrived at a *posta* (military station). 'I was here told of a fact, which, if I had not partly ocular proof, I could not credit. That in the previous night there had been a hailstorm (I saw lightning to the north) and the pieces of ice were as large as small apples and very hard. They fell with such force as to kill almost all the small animals. The men had already found 20 deers and I saw their fresh hides. . . . They thought they had seen about 15 dead ostriches; part of one I ate. . . . Many ducks and hawks were killed and ostriches were then running about evidently blind in one eye.'

Darwin arrived at Buenos Aires on 20 September 1833. He stayed with an English merchant, Mr Lumb, where 'I soon enjoyed all the comforts of an English home.' A week later he set out on his third expedition—Buenos Aires to Santa Fé on the Rio Parena, a distance of 300 miles. This excursion was particularly important because during the course of it he came across large numbers of fossil bones. He deduced that an open savannah type of country, rather than dense tropical forest, had been the home of the large extinct animals of the past.

Bivouac at the head of Port Desire Inlet, Christmas 1833

On the first day he rode eighty miles, yet 'with a burning sun, was but little fatigued'. Nearer Santa Fé 'there was a spectacle which my Gaucho looked at with great satisfaction, viz the skeleton with the dried skin hanging to the bones, of an Indian suspended to a tree'. Summary justice of this kind was the rule in Argentina.

Darwin had an attack of fever at Santa Fé which lasted only about three days but was sufficiently severe to make him change his plans and return by boat down the Rio Parena to rejoin the *Beagle*. Jaguars (or tigers as they were locally called) were common. 'All pleasure of wandering about the Islands is destroyed by fear of tigres.' Insects were equally distractive of pleasures. 'The mosquitoes very troublesome. I exposed my hand for five minutes. It was black with them: I do not think there could have been less than fifty, all busy with sucking.' The transmission of disease by this means had not occurred to anyone at this date.

On arrival at Buenos Aires he was once again delayed and became a virtual prisoner on the outskirts, because of yet another revolution. He did not reach the shelter of the *Beagle* until 4 November, and then only to learn that she was not to sail for the Horn until December. With the prospect of an unexpected month on his hands, Darwin immediately prepared to ride to the Rio Uruguay and its tributary the Rio Negro. He set out on this, his fourth, expedition on 14 November 1833. On the first day he remarks, referring to the peons, 'a naked man on a naked horse is a very fine spectacle; I had no idea how well the two animals suited each other'.

The *Beagle* set sail for the last time from Rio Plata on 6 December 1833, and anchored off Port Desire on 24 December. It is here that Darwin obtained convincing proof of the elevation of the land in South America. On visiting a plain to the north of the town which was several hundred feet above sea-level, he notes, 'It is remarkable that on the surface of this plain there are shells of the same sort which now exist, and the muscles even with their blue colour': two days later he found similar evidence to the south of the town but with oyster-shells. 'Is not this important?' he asks, as proof that the land there had been beneath the sea 'within no great number of centuries'.

Once more they visited Tierra del Fuego, the home of Jemmy Button and his friends, as the *Beagle* proceeded southwards. In the space of a few months Jemmy Button had become unrecognizable. 'It was quite painful to behold him; thin, pale and without a remnant of clothes, excepting a bit of blanket round his waist'; and 'so ashamed of himself he turned his back to the ship. . . . I never saw so complete and grievous a change . . . we were rather surprised to find he had no wish to return to England.' As the *Beagle* set out for the East Falkland Island Jemmy lit a farewell signal fire.

Jemmy Button (*top*) in 1834, one year later than the drawings on p. 23, and his wife

Cordillera of the Andes as seen from Mystery Plain, near the Rio Santa Cruz

The *Beagle* returned to the mainland of Sonth America and was beached at the mouth of the Rio Santa Cruz for repairs to her keel, which had been damaged at Port Desire. FitzRoy had planned to explore the upper reaches of the river. To do this he and his party of twenty-five, including Darwin, manhandled three boats tied end-to-end a distance of 245 miles upstream. This took them thirteen days of hard pulling, each man with a rope attached to a collar. At their farthermost point, with the snow-capped peaks of the Cordilleras ahead of them, they were only some sixty miles from the Pacific. The return journey downstream took them no more than three days.

This, the Captain's expedition, was eventually to provide Darwin with important geological data, but at the time what he saw worried him: 'My great puzzle how a river could form so perfect a plain . . . draining of sea?' The animals were disappointing except the huge herds of guanacos—'guanacos sleep tail in centre, in same place on different nights; then dung and dust in saucer-shaped cavities'. He shot a condor with a wing span of eight feet. For Captain FitzRoy the expedition was a failure: for Darwin it had been 'most satisfactory from offering so excellent a section of the great modern formation of Patagonia'.

Into the Pacific   On 12 May 1834, the *Beagle* sailed on her final voyage south, having completed the charting of that interminable eastern coast of South America. She made the Pacific by way of the Straits of Magellan by 9 June. They anchored

The *Beagle* laid ashore for repairs to her keel, Rio Santa Cruz

The *Beagle* at the foot of Mount Sarmiento, at the Pacific end of the Straits of Magellan

beneath the magnificent Mount Sarmiento with blue glaciers running from the heights to the sea like 'great frozen niagaras'.

Valparaiso was reached at the end of July and for the first time in nearly three years Darwin met people with whom he could discuss geology. He immediately planned to climb the Andes—for the first time volcanoes were available for him to study near by—and became engrossed in the effects and origin of earthquakes. Everything he saw convinced him that the plains had arisen from what had previously been the bed of the ocean. He found recent shells at an elevation of 1,300 feet. Insects and higher animals were comparatively rare, which leads him to conclude, 'It seems not very improbable conjecture that the want of animals may be owing to none having been created since this country was raised from the sea'; in Darwin's terminology 'been created' was synonymous with 'having arisen', yet he continued for some time to think of 'areas of Creation'.

Case of beetles collected by Darwin during the voyage

The Benchuca bug
His expedition into the Andes and Santiago was cut short by an illness which struck him on 19 September. This was probably due to a *Salmonella*-typhoid type of infection. It has recently been suggested that at some period he also contracted Chagas' disease, a chronic infection producing lassitude and later affecting the heart but with an acute phase at the outset. Chagas' disease, endemic throughout much of South America, is caused by a trypanosome commonly found in armadillos which, of course, Darwin was collecting and whose flesh he was frequently eating. It is also found in up to seventy per cent of the human population in certain parts of South America.

Chagas' disease is carried by certain reduviid bugs: in particular the Great Black Bug of the Pampas, the Benchuca or 'Barberio', which lives commonly in mud huts and the burrows of armadillos. A week previously Darwin had in fact, because of continual rain, to spend five days in one 'of a square of hovels, each with a table and stool'. We also know for certain that Darwin came across the Benchuca in Chile. At a later date (26 March 1835), on his Mendoza expedition, he writes in his journal, 'At night I experienced an attack, and it deserves no less a name, of the Benchuca . . . it is most disgusting to feel soft, wingless insects about one inch long, crawling over one's body. Before sucking they are quite thin, but afterwards round and bloated with blood and in this state they are quite easily squashed. They are found in the northern part of Chile and Peru: one which I caught at Iquiqui was very empty: being placed on the table and though surrounded by people, if a finger was presented, its sucker was withdrawn and the bold insect began to draw blood. It was curious to watch the change in the size of the insect's body in less than ten minutes. There was no pain felt. This one meal kept the insect fed for four months; in a fortnight, however, it was ready, if allowed, to suck more blood.' The important thing is that he could have met an infected bug during his extended stay in South America, that subsequently he allowed the 'Barberio' to bite a fellow-officer, and that he must have kept one alive for four months. It seems likely that chronic Chagas' disease, together with the neurosis that he later developed, was responsible for the periods of lethargy, the constant ill-health, and the frequent heart trouble which beset him on his return to England and lasted for the rest of his life, though this is not accepted by all specialists.

Whatever the cause of the fever, Darwin was very ill as he struggled back to Valparaiso. 'At night I was exceedingly exhausted; but had the uncommon luck of obtaining some clean straw for my bed. . . . If I had been in England

Benchuca (*Triatoma infestans*), the Great Black Bug of the Pampas.
Actual length about one inch

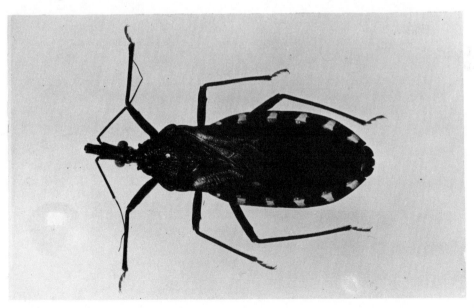

and very unwell, clean straw and stinking horse cloths would have been thought a very miserable bed.' To his sister Caroline he wrote, 'I had a long distance to travel and I suffered very much; at last I arrived here quite exhausted. . . . I consider myself very lucky to have reached this place.' Yet he continued his notebooks. His grand-daughter Nora Barlow, who has made a study of these, states, 'The hand-writing gets wild and straggling, but the notes continue and the evidence accumulates.'

From now on, in every letter he wrote, Darwin's great desire was to return home. As usually happens on long expeditions, this demand grew stronger each month: 'One whole night I tried to think over the pleasure of seeing Shrewsbury again.' Darwin was in the scientific doldrums.

Chile   These were rapidly dispersed on arrival at Concepción. On 20 February 1835, the great earthquake struck. Darwin was on shore lying down in a wood: 'It came on suddenly and lasted two minutes (but appeared much longer). . . .

Two pages from Darwin's notebooks, showing the straggling hand of a sick and exhausted man

Ruins of the Cathedral at Concepción after the great earthquake of 1835

The rocking was most sensible, the undulation appeared both to me and my servant to travel from the East. There was no difficulty in standing upright; but the motion made me giddy.' He later wrote to his sister Caroline, 'The town of Concepción is now nothing more than piles and lines of bricks, tiles and timbers.' Only reed huts escaped and 'these now are hired by the richest people'. The situation must undoubtedly have tickled the sense of humour of the democratic Darwin. It also gave him the opportunity of studying seismology in its acutest form. His account of the terrible scene is vivid and dramatic.

Returning to Valparaiso, Darwin set out on his seventh expedition, to Mendoza and Santiago. This was geologically most important to him. He records: 'It was the first view I ever saw which really resembled those pretty sections which geologists make of the inside of the earth.' He was accompanied by ten mules and 'a mare with a little bell round her neck: she is a sort of step-mother to the whole troup'. He seems to have made a complete recovery from his recent illness. He ascended the Andes to a height of 10,000 feet and more. He scoffs at the air hunger, or 'puna', as Chileños call it, which he met at this height. 'The only sensation I experienced was a slight tightness over the head and chest.'

Back at Valparaiso on 9 April he felt ill and miserable. To his sister Susan, however, a few days later he writes, 'Since leaving England I have never made so successful a journey; it has, however, been very expensive. I am sure my father would not regret it if he could know how deeply I have enjoyed it. It was something more than enjoyment: I cannot express the delight which I felt at such a winding up of all my Geology in South America: I literally could hardly sleep at night through thinking of my day's work.'

Within a week, however, he had set off on his last and longest expedition. This took him north to Copiapó, a distance of between 400 and 500 miles, where the *Beagle* was to pick him up two months later: for most of the trip he was entirely engrossed with geology. By the time he reached his destination he had accumulated 169 neatly labelled geological specimens: no mean load to carry on mules. Though he experienced severe cold sleeping out at night, there is no mention of ill-health. On one occasion he was in the saddle for twelve hours at a stretch.

He said farewell to Chile on 6 July. He had been away from home for over three and a half years: from now on it becomes clearer almost daily that his one desire is to get back. Peru was a waste of time because the political situation at Lima prevented him from going out into the country, but *en route* there in the *Beagle* he had once again been taking daily soundings by sinking a line with a lead attached: his thoughts were again concentrating on the formation of coral reefs. He could not agree with Lyell's explanation that they represented coral-encrusted rims of volcanic craters barely submerged. By now he had accumulated sufficient evidence to be certain of the upward and downward movements in the crust of the earth in this part of the world. Coral reefs and islands, according to Darwin, were born in shallow seas which subsequently sank. This is still valid today for the great majority of cases.

On 7 September 1835, the *Beagle* sailed for the archipelago of the Galápagos, destined to become the real turning-point in Darwin's life. Darwin had been primarily interested in geology. However, as soon as the ship reached the archipelago it is clear that he switched his main interest to biology: he noted that the flora and fauna had a certain similarity to those of South America. He was struck by the way the Spaniards could recognize from which island a tortoise had been collected. But the full significance of why the finch species

Galápagos Islands

Male marine iguana
on Narborough Island
in the Galápagos

Four different Galápagos finches—a striking example of the divergence of one species

which he collected were different did not immediately become apparent to him, nor the mocking-birds which again, though similar to South American mainland species, were specialized: two very different families of birds and both diverging.

Only later did he realize the full implications of his discoveries. Not only was each island populated by a different species of finch, which must have been derived from a common ancestor, but on a single island distinct species had exploited different biological niches. Some had become adapted to insect feeding, others had powerful beaks for seed eating. Yet, at that time, in one of his ornithological notebooks he wrote, 'when I see these Islands in sight of each other and possessed of but a scanty stock of animals, tennanted by these birds but slightly different in structure and filling the same place in nature, I must suspect they are only varieties. . . . If there is the slightest foundation for these remarks, the Zoology of archipelagoes will be well worth examining for such facts would undermine the stability of species.' He had begun to assimilate his data in a theory of evolutionary transformation. It was many years, however, before he was prepared to put these ideas into print, when he saw that the Galápagos facts could form the basis of his new theories on the mutability of species. Just over four weeks were spent in surveying the various Galápagos Islands—in future to be looked upon as one of the most decisive months in Darwin's life.

The ten days he spent at Tahiti are described in a letter to his sister Caroline (27 December 1835). 'The kind simple manners of the half-civilized natives are in harmony with the wild and beautiful scenery. I made a little excursion of three days into the Central Mountains. . . . Yet the woods cannot be compared to the forests of Brazil. . . . I would not exchange the memory of the first six months, not for five times the length of anticipated pleasures.' He was suffering from chronic overdoses of scientific data which he was unable to digest, and he became acutely aware of this during the long sea voyages when he attempted to write up the back-log of the journal.

Christmas Day 1835 was spent in New Zealand. Though there is no note-book available for this visit, Darwin's journal records it at some length. He found the native Maoris dirty and cunning in contrast to the excellent qualities of the Tahitians. 'One glance at their respective expressions, brings conviction to the mind that one is a savage, the other a civilized man. . . . There is absent that charming simplicity which is found at Tahiti.' He commends the missionaries in each place for the good work they are doing. At this stage of his life Darwin in fact is obsessed with the benefits conferred by missionaries. One of his first reports on the voyage appeared in the South African *Christian Recorder* (September 1836): 'On the whole, balancing all that we have heard and all that we ourselves have seen concerning the missionaries in the Pacific, we are very much satisfied that they thoroughly deserve the warmest support not only of individuals, but of the British Government.' This was signed jointly by Robert FitzRoy and Charles Darwin.

New Zealand

Maori natives of New Zealand, drawn by Captain FitzRoy

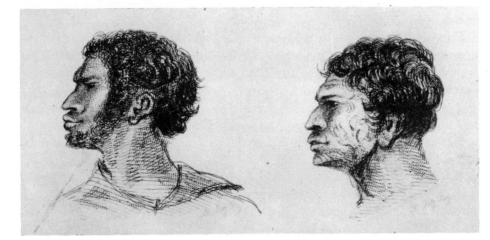

The duck-billed playtpus (*Ornithorhynchus*), a primitive egg-laying mammal

Australia   The *Beagle* reached Australia on 12 January 1836, after entering the fifth year of her voyage. 'My first feeling was to congratulate myself that I was born an Englishman.' Once again there is little in the notebooks. He remarks on the toll taken by European diseases such as measles among the aborigines, and the ill-effects of spirits on them: the infant mortality rate was particularly high owing to 'the wandering habits of these peoples'.

Darwin forecast the gradual extinction of wild animals. He was fortunate enough to see a duck-billed platypus one evening at dusk 'playing about the surface of the water'. He must have been confronted by many marsupial mammals, such as marsupial wolves and ant-eaters, for he records, 'a little time before this I had been lying on a sunny bank and was reflecting on the strange character of the animals of this country as compared to the rest of the world. An unbeliever in everything beyond his own reason might exclaim "Surely two distinct Creators must have been at work; their object however has been the same and certainly the end in each case is complete."' He continues, 'Now what would a disbeliever say to this? Would any two workmen ever hit on so beautiful, so simple and yet so artificial a contrivance? It cannot be thought so. The one hand has surely worked throughout the Universe.' By now Darwin was questioning the whole mechanism of Creation. Why should two so superficially similar creatures as the Australian and European wolves arise by such different paths?

They set sail on 14 March. 'Farewell Australia, you are a rising infant and doubtless some day will reign a great princess in the south; but you are too great and ambitious for affection, yet not great enough for respect; I leave your shores without sorrow or regret.'

46

Cocos Islands gave Darwin a further opportunity of developing his views on the origin of coral reefs. 'Every single atom [of rock fragments] bears the stamp of having been subjected to the power of organic arrangement.' 'Under this view, we must look at a lagoon island as a monument raised by myriads of tiny architects, to mark the spot where the former land lies buried in the depths of the ocean.' In this one vivid sentence he epitomizes his new theory.

After calling at Mauritius and the Cape of Good Hope, the *Beagle* left for her voyage north via St Helena and Ascension Islands. Darwin was now completely stale; his scientific data were getting out of hand. His sole intention was to write up his journal and prepare scientific papers during the long sail home.

The *Beagle*, alas, had to return unexpectedly across the South Atlantic to Bahia, their first port of call in South America four and a half years previously. She had now completed her circumnavigation of the globe. The visit momentarily rekindled some of Darwin's earlier enthusiasm. 'The land is one great, wild, untidy, luxuriant hothouse, which nature made for her menagerie,' he wrote, but his heart was set on home and his deeper feelings were expressed when he wrote, 'steered, thanks to God, a direct course for England'.

En route, Darwin reflected on the benefits and disadvantages he had received

Darwin concluded that the various kinds of coral island were the result of the gradual submergence of the island, by subsidence of the land (or by a rise in sea-level)

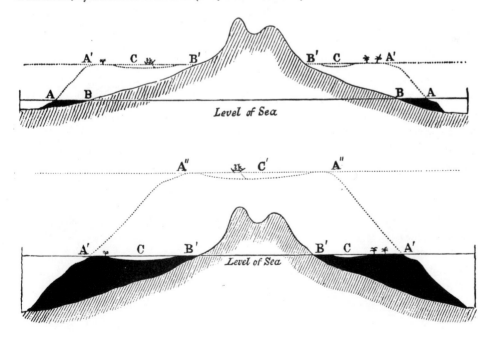

Darwin's microscope, still to be seen at Down House. On the *Beagle* voyage he had a portable instrument of lower power, in a travelling-case

from the voyage. 'If a person should ask me for advice before undertaking a long voyage, my answer would depend upon his possessing a decided taste for some branch of knowledge which could, by such a means, be acquired.' 'It is necessary to look forward to a harvest however distant it may be, when some fruit will be reaped, some good effected.' 'If a person suffer much from sea-sickness let him weigh it heavily in the balance.' 'Amongst the scenes which are deeply impressed on my mind, none exceed in sublimity the primaeval Forests, undefaced by the hand of Man, whether those of Brazil . . . or those of Tierra del Fuego, where death and decay prevail. Both are temples filled with the various productions of the God of Nature. No-one can stand unmoved in these solitudes, without feeling that there is more in man than the mere breath of his body.'

The *Beagle* tied up at Falmouth on 2 October 1836. Two days later Darwin was home at Shrewsbury, the first time for 'five years and two days'. His first wish was to justify his actions to his father. He was fortified in this by having received a letter at Ascension, where he learnt that 'Sedgwick had called on my Father and said that I should take a place among the leading scientific men.' Darwin records, 'that my mind became developed through my pursuits during the Voyage is rendered probable by a remark made by my Father . . . for on first seeing me after the Voyage, he turned round to my sisters and exclaimed, "Why, the shape of his head is quite altered"'

From now on he was to be accepted on his own merits.

Shrewsbury: the Old School playing-field and the Welsh Bridge

THE SYNTHESIS: 1836–1882

'Looking backward I can now perceive how my love for Science gradually preponderated over every other taste.'
'But I was also ambitious to take a fair place among scientific men.'
'I did not care much about the general public . . . and I am sure that I have never turned one inch out of my course to gain fame.' (*Autobiography*, 1887)

AFTER A HAPPY REUNION with his own family and his Wedgwood cousins, and several further visits to Shrewsbury and Maer, Darwin spent three months in lodgings at Cambridge, in touch with Henslow and the Professor of Geology, and then settled into lodgings in Great Marlborough Street in London, with Covington, late 'fiddler and boy to Poop Cabin' on the *Beagle*, as his assistant and secretary.

After sorting out his huge collections, helped by the same Professor Owen who later was to become his bitterest scientific enemy, he arranged for leading

Sir Richard Owen

specialists (such as Owen for fossil mammals, and Gould for birds) to describe them for publication, under his editorship, in the official *Zoology of the Voyage of the 'Beagle'*. Meanwhile, in a bare six months, he wrote his own account of the voyage, the famous *Journal of Researches*, which proved to be one of the best travel books ever written, full of general as well as scientific interest. The great von Humboldt was lavish in praise of Darwin's descriptions of tropical nature.

The 'parallel roads'
of Glen Roy

Once this was off his chest, Darwin started on three important books concerned with his own geological studies on the voyage—*Coral Reefs* (published
in 1842), *Volcanic Islands* (1844), and *Geological Observations on South America*
(1846). Meanwhile, early in 1838, he took on the Secretaryship of the Geological
Society, a post which he disliked, but through his three-year tenure of which he
firmly established his reputation as a geologist. He also started work on the
strange 'parallel roads' of Glen Roy in Scotland, and in 1839 published his
conclusion that they were marine beaches formed as a result of subsidence of the
land. This was one of the very few occasions where Darwin's scientific conclusions were wholly erroneous; in point of fact the roads originated as beaches
in a dammed-up glacial lake. His disillusionment must have helped to make
him over-cautious about the publication of his subsequent work. He certainly
learnt a lesson from his rashness—never again would he draw conclusions before
testing them against a vast body of facts collected for this very purpose.

Sir Joseph Hooker

During these years of great activity he met many leading scientists. The two most important for his future work were Sir Charles Lyell and Sir Joseph Hooker. Lyell was the acknowledged leader of geology in Britain, and his theory of uniformitarianism, which relied on the long-continued operation of processes now observable to explain all geological phenomena, was taken over by Darwin as the basis for his explanation of biological phenomena. However, Darwin radically transformed it by making it dynamic. Lyell's uniformitarianism denied the possibility of progressive change in organisms: Darwin's extension of it, to include the principle of natural selection, explained progressive change and indeed made it inevitable. Hooker was a younger man, of great energy and with vast botanical knowledge. He and Darwin struck up a firm friendship, and for years he was the only man to whom Darwin confided his ideas about evolution by natural selection.

'My theory'   By the end of the *Beagle*'s voyage, Darwin had become convinced that species were not immutable, but on the contrary could and did undergo change and transmutation, or as we say today, evolve; and furthermore that the change might be of large extent, transforming a species not merely into a very similar new species, but into a quite distinct new type or types, with markedly different

Sir Charles Lyell

structure and mode of life, as he was convinced had happened with the Galá-pagos finches, and on a still larger scale, both of time and place, with the armadillo-like creatures of South America.

In July 1837, after nine months occupied with his collections and the urgent aftermath of the voyage, he started a series of notebooks on the subject which he called *The Transmutation of Species*. A bare fifteen months later, he not only had become still more firmly convinced of the fact of transmutation but had built up a theory of how transmutation was brought about—the theory of evolution by natural selection—which remains to this day as the basic principle of bio-logical science.

It is interesting to follow in the notebooks his step-by-step progress, and to see how many and how diverse were the building-blocks out of which he was eventually able to construct his comprehensive theory.

He noted that sexual reproduction leads to more variation than does asexual or parthenogenetic; that much observable variation is heritable; that it is not directed towards a goal or directly related to changes in the environment; and that variation is apparently unlimited in extent. On the other hand, he recog-nized that species could remain constant over large areas, and that their incipient or full 'transmutation' would only occur as a result of physical isolation —as he had seen on the two sides of the Andes, or, still more strikingly, on the oceanic archipelago of the Galápagos.

He realized that a changed environment (including changes in the types and numbers of other organisms, whether competitors or predators, prey or food plants) would be necessary to cause the transmutation of an isolated population; that the animal types on oceanic islands would inevitably be allied to those of the nearest mainland; that the diversity of the types of finch on the Galápagos was due to their having become adapted for complementary ways of life (*adaptive niches* in modern terminology), and that the same principle applied to all adaptive radiations of a single ancestral type, even on the largest scale, like that of the marsupials in Australia, into swift herbivores, burrowers, arboreal forms, carnivores, and insectivores. In this and in other ways he laid the foundations for the modern science of ecology.

He had early realized that the structural resemblances between existing and fossil types in the same area must also be explained on the basis of common ancestry: as he put it in his pithy notebook style, 'in South America parent of all armadillos might be brother to Megatherium uncle now dead'. He saw that, on his theory, the result of large-scale transmutation will be, not just a vertical ladder of life, but an irregularly branching evolutionary tree, with extinction leading to gaps between the terminal twigs; and he soon grasped that 'simpler' types of animals with a lower degree of organization would inevitably persist alongside higher forms.

But the problems of adaptation remained. What mechanism would account for marvellous adaptations like those of woodpeckers for climbing trees, or of many plants for dispersal of their seeds through plumes to parachute them through the air or hooks to catch in animals' fur? Paley in his famous *Evidences of Christianity* had given a fine catalogue of such adaptations, but Darwin could not accept the Archdeacon's conclusion that they were evidence of separate acts of creation by Divine design. He had collected a mass of facts about the improvement of domesticated animals and cultivated plants, and, as he wrote later in his *Autobiography*, 'I soon perceived that selection was the keystone of man's success in making useful races of plants and animals.' Man's selection was also able to produce differences between the ancestral and the improved type as great as those found between related species in nature. But, he continued, 'How selection could be applied to organisms living in a state of nature remained for some time a mystery to me.'

Although he, like other naturalists of the period, recognized the fact of the struggle for existence; although he early saw that entire species could become extinct because of changes in the environment; and although by late September

The Thylacene or Tasmanian wolf: an example of evolutionary convergence

1838 he could note that 'forms slightly favoured' would get the upper hand and form new species, the problem remained a mystery until 3 October, when, happening 'to read for amusement Malthus on population' (we must be eternally grateful that Darwin had such a peculiar notion of amusement!) the solution flashed upon him—natural selection, a mechanism which inevitably tended to the preservation of favourable and the disappearance of unfavourable variations.

Malthus's basic point, that populations tend to increase in geometrical ratio unless checked, enabled Darwin to realize the intensity with which natural selection acts. As he wrote in his notebook at the time, 'one may say there is a force like a hundred thousand wedges trying to force every kind of structure into the gaps in the oeconomy of nature'.

'Here, then,' as he wrote later, 'I had at last got a theory by which to work' —'my theory', as he rightly called it, for though others had previously hit on one or other of its component elements, only Darwin had welded them all into a unified theory, and only this unified theory would account for the facts. He spent the rest of his life almost entirely in establishing the theory of evolution by natural selection on a firm basis, in following out its consequences and its implications, and in tracing the way it actually operated in nature.

Emma Darwin (*née* Wedgwood), after the portrait by George Richmond

Marriage   We know that Darwin immensely enjoyed visiting his Uncle Josiah Wedgwood's house at Maer, with its bevy of attractive daughters; but there is no evidence that he had fallen in love with any of them, nor indeed with anyone else, before his return from the *Beagle* voyage.

However, at the end of 1837 he solemnly (but perhaps not without a spark of humour in the background) drew up a kind of balance-sheet about matrimony, a longish document setting forth its advantages and disadvantages. Always over-cautious in money matters, he felt that if he married he would have to work for his living, he would have to give up travelling and would be unable to continue his study of species and their transmutation.

Among advantages he listed 'children—constant companion (friend in old age)—charms of music and female chitchat, good for one's health' (note this early preoccupation with health). But against these he listed 'terrible loss of

Charles Darwin at the
time of his marriage:
portrait by George Richmond

time' involved in social life in general and in being forced to visit and receive
relations; the expense and anxiety of children; and being tied to home.

Finally, however, his feelings get the better of him, and he wrote: 'My God,
it is intolerable to think of spending one's whole life like a neuter bee, working,
working, and nothing after all—No, no, won't do—Imagine living all one's
day solitarily in smoky dirty London—only picture to yourself a nice soft wife
on a sofa with good fire, and books and music perhaps. . . . Marry—Marry—
Marry: Q.E.D.'

That he must have been deeply attached to Emma Wedgwood without
acknowledging it to himself is evidenced by the fact that, having thus proved
to his own satisfaction that he ought to marry, and after clearing up the scientific
aftermath of the voyage, he posted off to Maer, and two days later, on 11
November 1838, proposed to Emma and was accepted.

12 Upper Gower Street,
London: the Darwins' first home

He could not have made a happier marriage nor found a more suitable wife. Emma was a year older than Charles, pretty and attractive but sober-minded and resolute, intelligent and capable like all the Wedgwoods, quietly energetic, and devoutly religious.

After a happy week's holiday, Darwin returned to London, where he combined work on his notebooks with strenuous house-hunting. After looking over eight houses, he took 12 Upper Gower Street, apparently without consulting Emma, and moved into it with his papers and his assistant on New Year's Day 1839.

On 24 January he was elected a Fellow of the Royal Society; five days later

St Peter's Church, Maer, where Charles and Emma were married. In the background, the chimneys of Maer Hall, the Wedgwood home

he was married at Maer. Immediately afterwards he returned with his bride to London: there was no honeymoon—work had to go on. On his wedding day itself he made an entry in his *Species* Notebook about plant-breeding: 'Uncle John [who had come to Maer for the wedding] believes one single turnip in a garden is enough to spoil a bed of cauliflowers.' And as soon as the young couple had settled in, they set about the serious business of household shopping.

During the first year of his marriage, Darwin went out a good deal into London society, and made many friends, scientific and other; but by the autumn he stopped going to parties, because they tired him too much—the first signs of his chronic invalidism.

Down House   He decided to live in the country, and bought Down House, Downe. This was only nineteen miles from London, on the rolling northern slopes of the North Downs, in an area abounding in the orchids he later studied to such good effect. It was, and still almost is, in the heart of the country: Darwin wrote that 'its chief merit is its extreme rurality'. Here he could read, experiment, write, walk in the grounds or occasionally ride out of them, and enjoy the company of his wife and family, and the visits of a few friends like Joseph Hooker and T. H. Huxley. Darwin seems to have been very happy at Down, apart from his constant and often painful ill-health, which from time to time drove him to take refuge in some hydropathic establishment.

Darwin described it as a 'good, very ugly house'. Actually, though it has no pretensions to architectural style, it has real character. Darwin's grand-daughter Gwen Raverat, in her delightful *Period Piece*, describes it as spacious and under-furnished, the furniture 'ugly in a way, but dignified and plain'. There was no running hot water, and no bathroom. Visitors can still see the house and garden

Down House: the front today

60

Down House: from the rear

almost as they were when Darwin died—his Old and New Studies, the drawingroom where he rested and was read to, played backgammon or listened to the piano, the greenhouses and hothouses where he experimented on his plants, the boxbordered kitchen garden. What particularly struck Gwen Raverat's imagination were the two great yew trees on the lawn, the big mulberry tree under the nursery window, the tumbledown gazebo hidden in a thicket, the Worm Stone on the lawn, against which Darwin measured the rate at which worm castings raised the level of the ground, and the Sandwalk along which he walked almost every day, through a door to a lonely meadow, round a wood he had planted himself, to a summerhouse, from which 'to this day you cannot see a single building anywhere', and back through a dark mossy path beset with huge beech trees.

On 27 December 1839, the first of their ten children had been born. This marked the beginning of Darwin's interest in human behaviour and the

Darwin with his eldest
son, William, born in 1839

expression of the emotions: he made all sorts of observations and experiments on
his infant son, and kept a detailed record of his progress. He was highly philo-
progenitive, to use the old-fashioned term, and was not only much concerned
about his children's health and future, but enjoyed playing and talking with
them and gave them great freedom. Once when Leonard (later President of the
Eugenics Society) was found enjoying the forbidden sport of jumping up and
down on the new sofa, his father merely said, 'Oh, Lenny, Lenny, that's against
all rules'; to which Lenny replied, 'I think you had better go out of the room.'
His biographer and son Francis (who helped him with his botanical work)
records that one of the boys offered him a whole sixpence to come and play with
them during working hours.

Emma Darwin and Lenny,
who was born in 1850

Darwin was the greatest amateur of all time—an amateur naturalist who
became a great scientist, and who luckily had enough money to be able to
dispense with a paid job. Down was the ideal home for such a man. His
method of work demanded the collection of vast stores of information on a
wide range of subjects, culled not only from books or scientific papers but from
the letters of a veritable army of correspondents in all parts of the world. Down
gave him leisure to amass the information, and space to store it in readily
available files.

His work also demanded constant observation and experiment on his own
part. For this, too, Down provided ample opportunity. The surrounding
countryside gave him opportunities for observations on general ecology, and on

Down House:
the lawn at the back,
with the big mulberry tree
under the nursery window

the adaptations of various species in nature. His own lawn gave him the possibility of measuring the activities of earthworms and their results. And his garden and his greenhouses gave him the opportunity to experiment on a number of important subjects, from cross-fertilization to plant movement, from heredity to insectivorous plants.

Down gave him rural peace and quiet, but was close enough to London to enable him to keep in touch with his friends and colleagues. At Down he was able to finish his great work and achieve his destiny.

The Royal College of Surgeons bought the estate some years ago, and have recently announced that, with the aid of a grant from the Nuffield Foundation, they are constructing in the grounds a centre for scientific research on two hundred monkeys—a most appropriate project for Darwin's home.

Thanks to the Royal College, Down House and its gardens are open to the public; yet only a handful of people visit it during the course of the year. Linnaeus's home at Hammarby in the country near Uppsala is a place of pilgrimage: visitors flock to it in bus-fuls from all over Sweden. Darwin was a greater scientist than Linnaeus—indeed one of the two greatest scientists that the world has produced and peculiarly English. Why should not Down become as much of a national shrine as Hammarby?

When he was a boy at Shrewsbury, Darwin's prowess as a runner was recognized; as an undergraduate at Cambridge he was robust, and enjoyed gay company and vigorous open-air pursuits, especially shooting. During the voyage of the *Beagle*, despite his one serious illness and several attacks of 'fever', he was extremely active, sometimes even out-riding the local guides. Yet from 1837 until he died in 1882, Darwin suffered constantly from ill-health. Going out to dinner or to a scientific meeting upset him for days. When his father died, he was too ill to accompany the funeral procession. In 1849, he wrote, 'I was not able to do anything one day out of three.' On at least six occasions he gave up working and went for a hydropathic cure to Malvern or elsewhere. For many years he made daily notes on his state of health, or rather ill-health. He became dependent on his wife, who during his later years never left him even for a night. Her protective solicitude seems to have fostered his desire to be protected. If she was the ideal nurse, he was the ideal invalid. As Gwen Raverat writes in *Period Piece*, 'At Down, ill-health was considered normal.'

Part of a sheet of Darwin's notes on his health. Half in code, half in clear, it gives a painfully vivid impression of chronic invalidism

However, we must remember that in spite of—or perhaps with the aid of—his invalidism, Darwin was able to get through a prodigious amount of work, to carry on a large correspondence, to take regular exercise, to welcome the visits of his friends, and to enjoy the company of his children.

What was the cause of this chronic ill-health, which lasted forty-five years and made Darwin a prisoner of his own invalidism? There are two main theories. One maintains that it was due to Chagas' disease, the other that it was psychoneurotic in origin. It is in fact probable that he suffered from both infection and neurosis. Many of his symptoms and much of his behaviour can most readily be interpreted as psychoneurotic. (This of course does not imply that he was hypochondriac or was in any way shamming illness: neurosis is something completely and terrifyingly real.) Certainly, once tiredness and unpleasant physical symptoms had developed, from whatever cause, it would be very easy for his subconscious to take refuge in invalidism in order to escape from the pursuit of social or professional duties, and to enable him to use as much as possible of his energy for what he rightly considered was his real work.

The predisposing cause of any psychoneurosis which Charles Darwin displayed seems to have been the conflict and emotional tension springing from his ambivalent relations with his father, Robert, whom he both revered and subconsciously resented. It is a fact that his father was always autocratic; he also seems to have been hostile to the whole idea of evolution (perhaps in reaction against the exposition of it by his own equally autocratic father Erasmus). This, together with Emma's deep-rooted dislike of such grievously unorthodox beliefs, goes a long way towards explaining Darwin's exaggerated diffidence about his own ideas on evolution, his reluctance to face up to their full implications, and his almost pathological resistance to publishing them before he felt he could overwhelm his critics with a mountainous array of buttressing facts. This trait may well have been reinforced by his recollection of his sad scientific error over the parallel roads of Glen Roy: he was not going to risk another failure.

'The Origin of Species' But whatever the reasons behind it, Darwin's reluctance to publish his theory, and even to spell it out on paper for his own satisfaction, clearly had some psychopathic basis. It was nearly two and three-quarter years after his note exulting in having at last got a satisfactory theory on which to work that, in his own words, 'I first allowed myself the satisfaction of writing a very brief abstract of my theory in pencil.' Darwin's idea of brevity can be gauged by the fact that the abstract was of thirty-five pages, and by the further fact that when at last he consented to write *The Origin of Species*, he always referred to it as an 'Essay', and originally wanted its title to be *An Abstract of an Essay on the Origin*

The Sandwalk, which Darwin often called his 'thinking path' ▶

Alfred Russel Wallace, 1853

of Species and Varieties through Natural Selection, but had to be over-ridden by his publisher's very natural objections.

Two years later he enlarged this abstract into an Essay of 230 pages, in which he included an astonishing volume of facts supporting his central theory. It is indeed an admirable preliminary version of *The Origin of Species*. There is only one important difference—the absence of any adequate treatment of the subject of evolutionary divergence, or, as Darwin put it, 'the tendency in organic beings descended from the same stock to diverge in character as they become modified'. This long puzzled Darwin, but it was not until much later, as he records in his *Autobiography*, that the solution came to him in a flash while he was out driving in his carriage near Down. (The solution, of course, was that the evolving stock is thereby advantaged by being able to exploit the diversity of the environment more fully.)

Although he thought highly enough of the Essay to write a formal letter to his wife asking her, in the event of his death, to arrange for its publication, with the co-operation of a suitable editor, he showed it to no one except Hooker, and for twelve further years, until 1856, merely continued with the amassing of ever more supporting facts.

Down House: the study

But on 14 May that year, urged by Hooker and by Lyell, who knew the importance of what Darwin was doing, he began to write a definitive work on the subject, to be entitled *Natural Selection*. This was to be on a monumental scale: he himself said it would have been four or five times as long as *The Origin*, which would have meant a book of at least 2,500 pages and three-quarters of a million words.

He set to the task with his usual industry. In just over two years he had finished ten long chapters, and was starting on an eleventh (on pigeons), when a bombshell arrived in the shape of a letter from Alfred Russel Wallace in the Moluccas, enclosing a short but perfect exposition of Darwin's own theory of evolution by natural selection, together with a request for comment and for help in getting it published.

What should he do? He felt it would be unfair to stand in Wallace's way, yet bitterly regretted the procrastination which was threatening to rob him of his long priority in the matter. He sought the advice of Lyell and Hooker, and

Wallace's bombshell: a Soviet artist's conception of the scene at Down House as Darwin read the letter to Hooker (*right*) and Lyell

agreed to their solution, that there should be joint publication. Accordingly, Wallace's paper and a brief summary of Darwin's own work were simultaneously presented at the meeting of the Linnaean Society on the memorable date of 1 July 1858, and were later published together as parts of a single communication in the Society's *Journal*.

Wallace's bombshell shattered Darwin's resistance to publishing his work, and he at once started on a book, using the material he had already prepared for the big book on natural selection. However, he soon found that his efforts at condensation were fruitless: the book continued to grow. So he set himself to write a moderate-sized abstract (as he called it) of his ideas and results. This was *The Origin of Species*, which he wrote in the astonishing time of thirteen months, in spite of seldom being free from pain for more than twenty minutes at a time.

Once his inhibitions had been overcome, books poured from his pen. The next two years were occupied in preparing a second and third edition of *The Origin*. In the twenty years after that, largely utilizing the materials he had accumulated for the big book that never saw the light, he published ten further books on evolutionary subjects, two of them of great length—an epoch-making contribution to man's understanding of himself and his planet.

We must now hark back from 1859 to 1846, when Darwin began to work on barnacles, a study which occupied his main energies for eight long years, and led to the publication of four monographs, two on living and two on fossil barnacles.

The fact that he had no inhibitions about publication in this field is a strong indication that his reluctance to publish anything about evolution sprang from some inner conflict about committing himself on this publicly controversial and privately painful subject. Indeed, it has been suggested with some plausibility that one reason (doubtless unconscious) for his taking up the study of barnacles was to have an excuse for putting off publishing his work and thoughts on evolution.

His interest in the group had originally been kindled by his discovery in Chile of a burrowing barnacle so different from all other barnacles that a new suborder had to be created for it; and the conscious reason he gave for devoting so much time to the subject was that he could not conscientiously go on speculating about the transmutation of species before he had found out for himself something about species in nature—what they really were, what was the difference between a species and a mere variety, how and why related species differed from each other, and so on. Be all this as it may, he threw himself wholeheartedly into the work—so wholeheartedly that one of his sons on a visit asked the children of the house, 'When does your father do his barnacles?'

Part of one of the few remaining leaves of the MS. of *The Origin of Species*

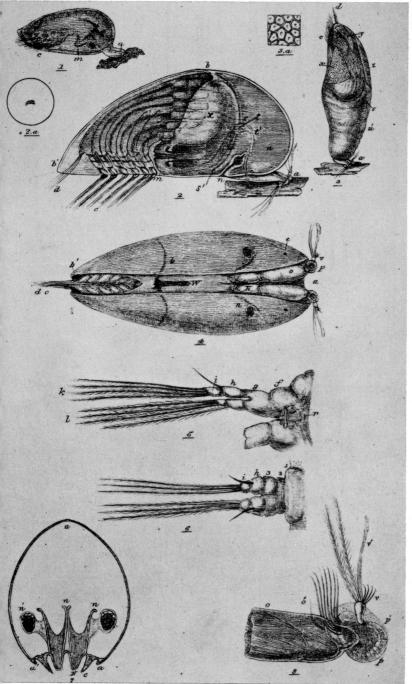

Last larval stages of the goose barnacle: a plate from one of Darwin's monographs

In point of fact, barnacles are of great evolutionary interest. Because of their shells and their sessile habits, they had usually been classified as Mollusca. However, in 1830 Vaughan Thompson made the remarkable discovery that they started life as free-swimming larvae built on the same plan as that of many crustaceans, thus demonstrating that barnacles were Crustacea which had come to adopt a sessile life as adults, or at least making it almost unthinkable that they would have been specially created in their present form.

Darwin himself discovered another fact of considerable importance—the existence in certain species of dwarf or complemental males ('little husbands', as he once called them) living like parasites in the mantle cavity of larger, hermaphrodite individuals. This confirmed Darwin's suspicion that some degree of cross-breeding was valuable, while the fact that the male organs of the hermaphrodites were much reduced in size strengthened his belief that transmutation of type would always be gradual.

ON

THE ORIGIN OF SPECIES

BY MEANS OF NATURAL SELECTION,

OR THE

PRESERVATION OF FAVOURED RACES IN THE STRUGGLE
FOR LIFE.

By CHARLES DARWIN, M.A.,
FELLOW OF THE ROYAL, GEOLOGICAL, LINNÆAN, ETC., SOCIETIES;
AUTHOR OF 'JOURNAL OF RESEARCHES DURING H. M. S. BEAGLE'S VOYAGE
ROUND THE WORLD.'

LONDON:
JOHN MURRAY, ALBEMARLE STREET.
1859.

The right of Translation is reserved.

The Origin of Species:
title-page of the first edition

Another valuable finding was the great degree of variability displayed by so many barnacle species. High variability was a prerequisite for Darwin's theory, for without it selection could achieve nothing. Variability is the raw material of evolution: natural selection utilizes and directs it to produce biologically desirable change. Thus, though the time that Darwin spent on his barnacles may have been excessive, it was certainly not wasted.

Something of the same sort may be said of the twenty-year delay in publishing his theory of evolution by natural selection. Wallace's paper of 1858 was under twelve pages long, and was confined to general argument, without any supporting factual evidence. If Darwin had published a similar short and theoretical paper in 1838, his general conclusions, in spite of their originality and immense importance, would almost certainly have been still-born. Before becoming acceptable to biologists, and still more to the general educated public, the idea of evolution as a natural and gradual process had to be buttressed with a multitude of hard facts, and the novel principle of natural selection had to be thoroughly analysed and its implications fully worked out. The Essay of 1844 would have largely met these requirements: but it needed the rise of younger biologists like Hooker, Alfred Newton and, above all, Huxley to ensure professional support for Darwin's revolutionary views.

On the other hand, considerable further delay might well have led to his missing the evolutionary bus. Certainly, it would have been most unfortunate if Darwin had insisted on finishing his enormous work on natural selection before publishing anything at all on evolution. The essential argument would have been obscured by the multitude of facts, and few people, certainly very few laymen, would have had the patience to read it.

Thus science owes a great debt to Alfred Russel Wallace, and to the malarial parasite which gave him an enforced rest from his collecting labours and so enabled him to think. For without the results of that brilliant spasm of thought, *The Origin of Species* would never have been written.

Reception of   Darwin was so diffident about the merits of his 'little work', as he called *The*
'The Origin'   *Origin*, that he wrote to John Murray, his faithful publisher, to tell him 'if you feel bound . . . to say in clearest terms that . . . you do not think it likely to have a remunerative sale, I completely and explicitly free you from your offer'.

In point of fact, *The Origin* was extremely remunerative. The first edition of 1,250 copies at fifteen shillings was bought up on the day of publication. A second edition was published six weeks later, and from then on a stream of new and revised editions had to be prepared, and continued to sell.

The Origin was also an admirably organized work, in which Darwin buttressed his novel and illuminating hypothesis with a powerful array of facts, and explored the implications of the theory of transformation by natural selection into every field of evolutionary biology—the divergence of organisms into a multitude of varied types, the specialized improvement and general advance of life, the change of function of organs, adaptation, stability, and extinction. He even pointed out the possibility of a human population explosion, and elsewhere foreshadowed present-day views on the origin of life.

The immediate success of the book was due partly to the lucky accident that, owing to the illness of its usual scientific reviewer, *The Times* gave the book to T. H. Huxley to review. He was bowled over by the idea of natural selection —a stroke of genius, he felt, comparable to Columbus's method of dealing with eggs. He exclaimed, 'How extremely stupid not to have thought of that!' and gave the book a long and appreciative review.

Huxley was the most brilliant zoologist in England, Hooker the best botanist, and Lyell the greatest geologist; and they all supported *The Origin*, as did Herbert Spencer, Sir John Lubbock (later Lord Avebury), Canon Tristram, the zoologist of the Bible, Alfred Newton, the rising young ornithologist, and Charles Kingsley, the Broad Church clergyman and novelist.

But Darwin did not have it all his own way among his scientific colleagues. Philip Gosse, the naturalist father in Edmund Gosse's *Father and Son*, was a Plymouth Brother, and though he had to acknowledge the validity of Darwin's

Thomas Henry Huxley in 1857, at the age of thirty-two

Sir Richard Owen: cartoon from *Vanity Fair*

facts he could not bring himself to give up the creationism which his religious orthodoxy demanded. Accordingly he wrote an extraordinary book called *Omphalos*, in which he maintained that the world and all it contained must have been created perfect—Adam and Eve with the navels they would have had if they had been born in the natural way, the trees with the annual rings they would have had if they had grown from seed, the rocks with all the fossils that would have been entombed in them if the world had existed for millions of years. He was sadly disappointed when the book fell completely flat.

Professor Adam Sedgwick, the veteran geologist with whom Darwin had once made a geological excursion in Wales, was horrified, and attacked him—quite unfairly—for having deserted the true scientific method of Baconian induction.

But Darwin's most dangerous scientific opponent was Richard Owen. Owen was an outstanding comparative anatomist and palaeontologist, and had been very friendly with Darwin in earlier days. But he was a disciple of Cuvier, the leading opponent of transmutation, and also a jealous and, as it proved, an unscrupulous man. He wrote a long, hostile, and—typically of him—anonymous review of *The Origin*, which Darwin himself described as 'extremely malignant and clever'.

Of course there was widespread religious opposition to Darwin's ideas. The only reference in *The Origin* to what Darwin later called the descent of man is the masterpiece of understatement in the Conclusion, that when his or analogous views on the origin of species come to be generally admitted, 'light will be thrown on the origin of man and his history'. In spite of this it was immediately obvious to any intelligent person that Darwin's general conclusions were quite incompatible with current Christian doctrine about the creation, about the descent of man from the single couple Adam and Eve, about the Fall, and about the time-scale of planetary and human events. No wonder that a clergyman warned Henry Trimen, the botanist, that Darwin was the most dangerous man in England, and that for a Presbyterian professional geologist like Adam White *The Origin* was a lapse into pernicious error.

Owen was the scientific *éminence grise* behind this religious opposition. It was he who briefed Bishop Wilberforce, nicknamed 'Soapy Sam', for that famous debate on evolution at the Oxford meeting of the British Association in 1860. Unfortunately for Owen and the Bishop, but fortunately for Darwin and biological science, T. H. Huxley, still only thirty-five but at the height of his powers, was prevailed on to speak, and completely routed the Bishop and his contingent of orthodox camp-followers.

The Oxford meeting

At an earlier session, Owen's anti-Darwinian statement that the brain of the gorilla differed more from that of man than it did from those of the lowest monkeys had been met by a direct contradiction from Huxley, who had been studying this very point for nearly two years. This aroused little interest, but a later general debate on Darwin's views at which Bishop Wilberforce was billed to speak attracted a large crowd. Huxley was sure that Wilberforce would appeal to prejudice in this mixed audience, and had intended to leave that morning, but was persuaded to stay and support Darwin's cause if need be. The Bishop, after a display of brilliant but unfair eloquence, turned to Huxley and asked whether it was through his grandfather or his grandmother that he claimed descent from a monkey. At this Huxley muttered, 'The Lord hath delivered him into mine hands'; and then, after an equally brilliant but scientifically compelling answer to the Bishop's main thesis, quietly and deliberately said something like this (the precise wording was never recorded): that if he had to choose between a poor ape for an ancestor and a man highly endowed by nature and of great influence, who used those gifts to introduce ridicule into a scientific discussion and to discredit humble seekers after truth, he would affirm his preference for the ape. The effect was so great that one lady fainted in the general commotion. He then further demolished the Bishop's scientific arguments. The Bishop knew when he was beaten and did not reply.

Darwin: 'How durst you attack a live bishop in that fashion?'

Ernst Haeckel,
famous biologist and popularizer:
Darwin's earliest supporter in Germany

This marked the turning-point of the dispute in Britain. Though the attacks continued, they were more and more successfully repelled, largely by Huxley, who christened himself Darwin's bulldog.

The scientific battle was quickly won in other countries too. In the United States the creationist Louis Agassiz, in spite of his great reputation, failed to convince his younger colleagues. In Germany the leading biologists soon rallied to Darwin's side, and Haeckel took on a similar role to Huxley's in Britain. The same sort of thing happened in most other Western countries, including Russia; though France, whose scientific patriotism found it hard to abandon the views of their two biological heroes, Cuvier and Lamarck, lagged markedly behind. In 1872 a proposal to elect Darwin as an Honorary Member to the zoological section of the French Academy was decisively rejected; it was not until 1878 that he got in, and then (to his considerable amusement) only through the botanical door.

Das Kapital.

Kritik der politischen Oekonomie.

Von

Karl Marx.

Erster Band.

Buch I: Der Produktionsprocess des Kapitals.

Zweite verbesserte Auflage.

Das Recht der Uebersetzung wird vorbehalten.

Hamburg

Verlag von Otto Meissner.

1872.

Second edition of
Das Kapital,
inscribed by Karl Marx
to Darwin

Karl Marx venerated Darwin and wanted to dedicate the English translation of *Das Kapital* to him—a request which was courteously refused. Darwin has become an intellectual hero in the Soviet Union. There is a splendid Darwin Museum in Moscow, and the Soviet authorities struck a special Darwin medal in honour of the centenary of *The Origin*. T. H. Huxley, on the other hand, has never found such favour in Soviet Russia, because of his refusal to adopt an atheist instead of an agnostic position.

Medal struck in Moscow
in commemoration of the
centenary of *The Origin of Species*

In some quarters, especially in Germany, the attempt was made to apply
Darwinian concepts, such as the struggle for existence and the survival of the
fittest, directly to human affairs, under the guise of 'social Darwinism'. 'Social
Darwinism' was of course only a pseudo-science, and its extrapolations from
biology to social science and politics were quite unjustified. They led to the
glorification of free enterprise, *laissez faire* economics and war, to an unscientific
eugenics and racism, and eventually to Hitler and Nazi ideology.

Within a dozen years from the publication of *The Origin*, biology had become
an evolutionary science, though by a strange irony most biologists concentrated
merely on comparative anatomy and embryology, with the cultivation of forests
of evolutionary trees. Only Darwin himself, together with a few others like
Wallace, Bates, Fritz Müller, Cope, and Marsh, continued to pursue the study
of scientific natural history.

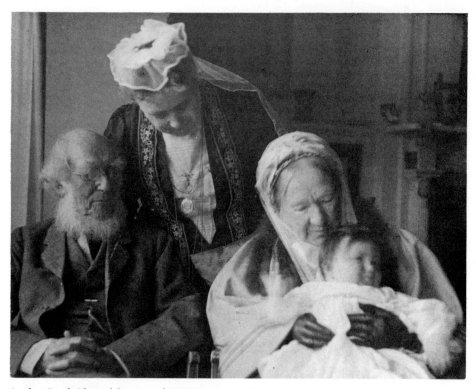

At the Cambridge celebration of the Centenary of Darwin's birth, in 1909: *l. to r.*, Sir Joseph Hooker, Lady Hooker, Mrs T. H. Huxley, Ursula Darwin

A splendid centenary commemoration of Darwin's birth was held in Cam-bridge in 1909, graced by the presence of Sir Joseph Hooker and T. H. Huxley's widow. In 1958 the centenary of the Darwin–Wallace paper was commemorated in London at the International Congress of Zoology, and also elsewhere; and in 1959 there were centenary celebrations of the publication of *The Origin* all over the world. The most notable was at the University of Chicago, where for the first time anthropologists and social scientists joined with biologists, cosmologists, and other natural scientists to discuss cultural or psychosocial evolution and the application of evolutionary ideas to human life and affairs. Socially, the high point of the celebration was the performance of a musical comedy on Darwin and Darwinism, entitled *Time Will Tell*, written, composed, and acted by members of the university staff. The finale sung by a chorus of ladies, clergymen, dons, and undergraduates, who had been at the Huxley–Wilberforce debate, ran as follows:

A hundred years hence
Will Darwin make sense
To the likes of us
Who are on the fence?
Will a century make a difference?
Only time will tell.

Well, time has told, and it has made a difference to the whole world, and to man's way of thinking about himself and his destiny.

Of the ten biological books which Darwin published after 1859, six were concerned with particular botanical problems, like climbing plants, insectivorous plants, and devices for securing cross-pollination; one was on the special ecological problem of the effect of earthworms on the environment; and three were major contributions to the general subject of evolution, dealing with variation, with the origins of man (strangely coupled with sexual selection), and with the expression of the emotions. These were largely amplifications of the material he had collected and in part written up for his great unpublished book on natural selection, and served to support and extend *The Origin* in various important ways. But he felt the need for recasting his ideas and for collecting a further mass of facts in support of them, so that it was not until 1868, nine years after the publication of *The Origin*, that the first of the great trio was published. *'Variation under Domestication'*

This was entitled *The Variation of Animals and Plants under Domestication*. Like all Darwin's later books, it was the unfolding of a germ that had long existed in his mind. Already in 1837 he had realized that man's artificial selection could produce radical changes in domestic animals and cultivated plants, but

The high spot of the Chicago centennial's musical comedy, *Time Will Tell*. Professor Huxley answers the Bishop—in song

The clearest case of variation produced by artificial selection.
(*Left*): the wild rock pigeon, *Columba livia*, from which such different varieties as (*opposite*) the carrier pigeon and the pouter pigeon were derived

that it could only do so on the basis of a large degree of variation; and the same held for the principle of natural selection, which he discovered in the following year. Without variability as its raw material, no amount of selection, whether human or natural, could achieve anything. In this book, he set out to document these conclusions, by adducing evidence for the occurrence of large-scale variation under domestication, and by giving examples of the amount of divergence from ancestral type that human selection could produce.

Already in 1856 he had employed domestic pigeons as the material of his choice to illustrate the latter point, partly because their origin from the wild rock pigeon *Columba livia* was undisputed, but mainly because their domestic breeds showed a greater range of diversity than those of any other animal. Accordingly he joined two pigeon-fanciers' clubs, kept all the important breeds he could secure, prepared their skeletons for study, and made crosses between them, crosses which in many cases reverted to the appearance and colour of the ancestral rock pigeon.

All these results he incorporated in the book, together with similar results, though on a smaller scale, on breeds of rabbits. He adduced a mass of supporting

evidence from ducks and horses, pigs and sheep, poultry and canaries, goldfish and silkworms; from domestic dogs (which he concluded had originated from different wild ancestors in different parts of the world); from domestic cats (whose relative uniformity he ascribed to their more intractable nature and habits); from the records of early domestication and cultivation in Mesopotamia and Egypt, India and China; and from what happens to domestic breeds when they are allowed to become secondarily wild or feral.

In addition he collected a large body of facts about the new variations occurring in domesticated species, including such phenomena as zebra-like stripes on the legs of foals in some horses, and what we should now call mutations with large effects, like the short legs of Ancon sheep.

Although Mendel's epoch-making work, proving the existence of non-blending inheritance for sharply distinct characters that we now know must have originated by mutation, was published in 1866, and although Darwin himself found similar sharp segregation of characters in some of his experimental sweet-pea crosses, he clung to the theory of blending inheritance. Furthermore, his firm belief in the gradualness of evolutionary change, a belief

Variation
in domestic poultry:
(*opposite*), Hamburgh fowl
and Polish fowl;
(*right*), Spanish fowl

which has been fully confirmed by all later work on the subject, led him to
discount the evolutionary importance of such sharply distinct characters and of
all 'sports' or mutations of large extent. On the other hand, he knew that man
had taken advantage of the Ancon mutation to breed a stock which could not
jump over walls or fences, and surmised that some breeds of dogs, like the pug,
might have originated as single mutational sports.

He also described and discussed such subjects as the results of cross-breeding;
the influence of the environment on variability, especially in plants; and the
direction of man's selection in plants—towards beauty in garden flowers, better
fruit in gooseberries, better seeds in cereals, better leaves in lettuces. A notable
section is devoted to what Darwin termed correlated variability, or con-
sequential variation as it is sometimes called today—variations which appear to
be the inevitable accompaniment or consequence of some other variation. Thus
absolutely larger individuals and species of deer have relatively as well as
absolutely larger antlers, four-horned sheep have coarse wool, and blue-eyed
white cats are almost invariably deaf.

Towards the end he introduced his theory of pangenesis, which was designed
to account for the multiple phenomena of heredity, variation, development,

regeneration, and the supposed inheritance of acquired characters, on the basis of hypothetical 'gemmules' budded off from all tissues of the organism and carried in the blood to the reproductive organs or wherever they were needed.

Darwin always felt the need for some theoretical basis for the better understanding of the facts he collected, and, in the absence of any contemporary knowledge about the mechanisms underlying reproduction and development, put forward this wholly hypothetical idea to satisfy that need. Not unnaturally, the hypothesis was quite erroneous. But one must admire Darwin's efforts to provide scientific comprehension of these difficult subjects, and must remember that the world had to wait over forty years for a satisfactory theory of heredity and nearly as long even for a satisfactory description of individual development, while a comprehensive theory of how development operates still eludes us.

In the middle decade of the nineteenth century it was virtually necessary for any general biologist to admit some inheritance of acquired characters. The remarkable fact remains that Darwin always relied on natural selection as by far the most important agency of evolutionary change. How delighted he would have been with the modern disproof of all kinds of Lamarckism, and with R. A. Fisher's rigorous demonstration that evolution could only occur on the basis of natural selection of particulate variations—i.e. small mutations of unit genes. Modern biologists, with negligible exceptions, are all neo-Darwinian selectionists.

The book *The Variation of Animals and Plants under Domestication* was a mighty effort for its time, and contains an astonishing store of facts about variation, its range and its limitations, the conditions which promote it, and the effects of artificial selection. In spite of its inevitable errors of interpretation, it can still be consulted with profit by the diligent biologist.

'The Descent of Man'

Darwin had intended to follow up *The Variation of Animals and Plants* with other volumes similarly expanding other themes in *The Origin* and utilizing the stores of material he had gathered for the big unfinished work on natural selection. But the writing of the book on variation proved so laborious and in a sense unrewarding that he turned to a new and more exciting theme—the descent of man.

Though he had thought about the subject ever since he first saw the Fuegian savages on the *Beagle* voyage, had amassed many facts bearing on it, and had dropped a number of hints about man's animal ancestry in *The Origin*, he had been content to assert, at the end of its final chapter, that, with the aid of his theory, 'light will be thrown on the origin of man and his history'.

In *The Descent of Man*, aided by T. H. Huxley's memorable book of 1863, *Evidences of Man's Place in Nature*, Darwin fulfilled his own prophecy in a remarkable way. After its publication in 1871, no serious biologist continued

Darwin never suggested that man had descended from an ape, but the idea afforded much mirth for lesser minds, as witness a cartoon from the *Hornet* of 22 March 1871

to believe that man was descended from a single couple created only a few thousand years ago; or questioned the view that man had originated by natural means—not from any existing ape or monkey, as some of Darwin's more stupid and unscrupulous critics asserted he had said, but from an ape-like primate, and before him from an animal which would have to be classified as belonging to the group of Old World monkeys. Not only that, but with astonishing acumen he deduced that man had probably originated in Africa, a conclusion which today, thanks to the discoveries of Broom and Dart and Leakey, has become a virtual certainty.

The great apes resemble man in structure, expression, and even in practising 'art'. An orang-utan with one of his paintings

Darwin began with the physical resemblances between man and the apes: resemblances in structural plan, in brain and sense-organs, in hair and facial musculature, in parasites, in proneness to various diseases, in being tailless but in possessing a vestigial tail as an embryo—a fact which provides the further demonstration that earlier human ancestors must have had functional tails. Another vestigial structure, the so-called 'Darwin's point' present in many human ears, apparently represents the infolded tip of an ancestral pointed ear like that of most quadrupeds.

He also stressed the resemblances in physiological plan—in reproduction, gestation, birth, lactation, and development. Even more important was the emphasis he laid on similarities in psychological characters, such as instincts and emotions, curiosity and sociality, and on the presence in apes and monkeys of the germs of distinctively human qualities like reason, imagination, and morality, germs which could readily have unfolded their full potentialities under the influence of natural selection and later of social pressure. With this he took the first steps towards establishing the study of comparative psychology and behaviour, or ethology as we now call it, as a science in its own right.

He of course stressed the fact that the obvious superiority of man's mental processes was a direct consequence of the remarkable increase in the size of his brain, from a mean volume of 650 c.c. in the largest ape, the gorilla, to about 1,400 c.c. in present-day man. It was only after his death that we have managed to discover the main intermediate steps in this process, from the African australopiths to primitive Java 'ape-man' and his further advance to Pekin man, and through the Old Stone Age to Neanderthal man and the modern-type man to whom we owe the world's first art.

He also accepted Wallace's conclusion of 1864 that this perfection of man's brain and mental faculties made further evolution of his body unnecessary: specialized tools and machines could function as extensions of his person, and were more efficient than any specialized bodily organ.

On the other hand Darwin's general preoccupation with the gradualness of evolution, and the importance, in the prevailing climate of opinion, of demonstrating that the final evolution of modern man from an ape-like ancestor could take, and must have taken, place gradually, by a series of quite small steps, led him (and generations of professional zoologists after him) to neglect and indeed even to fail to mention the fact of man's uniqueness, with all its consequences.

Man's uniqueness consists in his capacity for complex and abstract thinking, and his consequent possession of a symbolic method of communication. Animals communicate by sounds and gestures which act as signs of their emotional states; man alone has true speech with words for things and ideas.

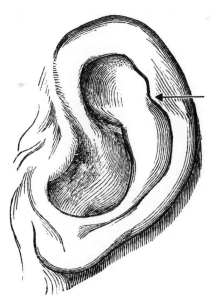

Darwin's point—an occasional vestige, Darwin suggested, of the pointed ears of man's early mammalian forebears

Australopithecus, an ape-like ancestor of man, lived and hunted a million years ago in Africa—a habitat suggested by Darwin in *The Descent of Man*

Man alone can express his state of mind in works of art and ritual celebrations and can formulate and order his experience in generalized statements and scientific laws. As a result, man possesses what amounts to a second mechanism of heredity. He can hand on his experience and its results cumulatively down the generations: he can transmit culture. As a further result, modern man's evolution has been and still is primarily cultural, concerned with changes in ideas and techniques, in social organization and artistic expression, and only secondarily biological, concerned with genetic changes in bodily or mental capacities.

Man, in fact, has embarked on a wholly new phase of evolution, the psycho-social phase, in which he has the responsibility for his own future evolution, and indeed for that of the whole planet. For this task, he must learn the rules of this new kind of evolution and study the mechanisms by which it operates. Though of course a knowledge of his animal origin and of the genetic mental and bodily capacities he has inherited from his ape-like progenitors is essential, it is unimportant compared with fuller knowledge of his cultural capacities and their possible realization in psychosocial organization.

But this in no way belittles Darwin's achievement. *The Descent of Man* was a milestone in scientific progress. As *The Origin* opened the door to the vast and varied fields of evolutionary biology, *The Descent of Man* opened the door to the study of man as a natural phenomenon.

The Descent of Man is really two books in one, as was indicated by the inclusion in its full title of the phrase '*and Selection in Relation to Sex*'. In point of fact, nearly three-quarters of it is devoted to sexual selection. By sexual selection Darwin meant the kind of selection which operates through some members of a species enjoying an advantage over others, not in regard to individual survival, but to mating and the propagation of their kind. It thus works entirely intra-specifically, between members of a single species; and most frequently intra-sexually, between the male members of the species. In other words, it is the result not of the struggle for existence in the usual sense, but of the struggle for reproduction.

Sexual selection

According to Darwin, it operates in two main ways—by combat or by display. Sexual selection by physical combat and the threat of combat charac-terizes most mammals, and leads, in the males of the species, to the development of increased size and strength (as in fur-seals, walruses, and sea-elephants), of

Where sexual selection operates by combat in polygamous species, male size has high selective value. The massive bulk of the male elephant seal is made even more formidable by an inflatable proboscis

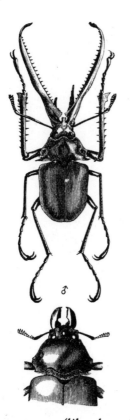

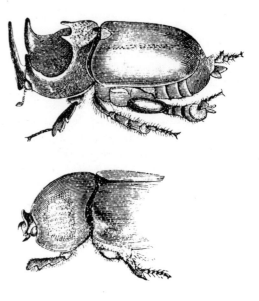

(*Left*) the male Chilean beetle *Chiasognathus grantii* has disproportionately long mandibles, probably for threat as much as actual fighting.
The large horns of the male beetle *Dipelicus* (*top*) serve the same purpose. (*Above*) The female, for comparison

weapons (like the enlarged canine teeth of male baboons, muntjac deer, and wild boars), and of devices to make the animal appear bigger or more formidable (like the manes of lions and bison, the white gums revealed by baring the teeth in some primates, and the inflatable proboscis of the sea-elephant).

Darwin applied the same reasoning to all other cases where the males alone possess weapons, like the huge jaws of stagbeetles and many other Coleoptera, and the enlarged claws of lobsters and many other Crustacea (though in this last group, many specialized male claws appear not to be mainly weapons in the strict sense, but organs for gripping and holding the female).

In polygamous mammals like sea-elephants the superiority of the males in size and strength is enormous. As Darwin pointed out, this is a natural consequence of their polygamy. The successful males will possess many females, the unsuccessful ones none; thus the intensity of selection for the characters making for success in fighting for a mate will be extremely high.

In birds, on the other hand, there is a preponderance of display. The males of many birds are much more brightly coloured than the females, their striking colours and patterns often restricted to specially developed parts of the plumage

Mutual display by a mated pair of great crested grebes

Combined vocal and visual display: the orange-coloured inflatable sacs of the male prairie chicken

(like the ruff and eartufts of the ruff, the special plumes of birds of paradise, or the gorget of various humming-birds). Furthermore, they indulge in elaborate displays in which the bright colours and special plumage are shown off as conspicuously as possible, whereas during the birds' normal activities they are inconspicuous and often tucked away out of sight.

Darwin believed that in these and the many other cases (as in lizards, fish, and spiders) in which the males are more brightly or strikingly patterned than the females, selection operates through female choice, the females consciously or unconsciously selecting the brightest and most striking males to mate with.

As in mammals, so in birds, polygamy puts a much greater premium on male success, and accordingly leads to the exaggeration of display characters, sometimes to an astonishing extent. Indeed, the gorgeous 'tail' or train of the male peacock and the incredible wings of the male Argus pheasant are so hypertrophied as to hamper their possessors' capacity for flight: yet so great is the advantage of success in mating that it is able to over-ride this handicap to survival in the ordinary business of life.

Darwin applied the same reasoning to male song, whether vocal as in most birds, or instrumental as in snipe, grasshoppers, and cicadas; the females, he

Darwin: a studio photograph
taken about 1856

supposed, preferred the best-endowed male singers. Today, new facts inevitably
unknown to Darwin make his theory untenable in its original form. Thus
the great majority of small (passerine) birds are monogamous, and display
by the male to the female does not begin until after the pair have joined
up for the season: so it can have nothing to do with the choice of a mate.
Actually it seems to serve mainly to stimulate and synchronize the act of
copulation.

In such species, the bright colours, the displays, and the striking songs of the
males are concerned primarily with the maintenance and defence of a territory,
where mating or nesting will later take place. They are on the one hand warn-
ings to rival males not to trespass, and advertisements to females that here is an
eligible home-site complete with potential mate.

In polygamous species with communal mating-grounds, like ruff, blackcock, or prairie chicken, there are two kinds of male display, one purely hostile and directed at any masculine rivals that approach a male's jealously guarded mating-station, the other stimulative and addressed to visiting hens. Only in such species do matters work out as Darwin supposed, by the females deliberately preferring one male to another.

Rather surprisingly, Darwin made no mention of the numerous cases (as in grebes, divers, herons, and pelicans) where both sexes possess striking ornaments which are only developed (or only used) in the breeding season, and employ them in mutual displays in which both birds take part, often playing identical roles. Such displays, we now know, not only function as stimulators and synchronizers of mating but create an emotional bond between the two birds, which serves to keep the pair together through the long period where both are needed to feed and guard the young.

This curious omission, I suspect, stems largely from Darwin's firm belief in female choice as the selective agent leading to male display characters, so that he neglected the cases of mutual display, or dismissed them as somehow irrelevant.

In the final chapter of the book, Darwin deals with sexual selection in man. He rightly points out that in the human species any deliberate mate-selection is of women by men, not the other way round, and indeed that it is female, not male characters which are concerned with differential success in mating and reproduction—characters like facial beauty, a good figure, smooth hairless skin, red lips, and shapely breasts. And of course women of every country deliberately attempt to enhance the efficacy of any natural characters of the sort by artificial means—rouge and lipstick, corsets and jewels, bustles and brassières.

Furthermore, however, Darwin points out that different races and cultural groups have different standards of human beauty and attractiveness. In some African races the women have enormous buttocks: in one tribe the chief selects his wives by arranging the women in line and choosing those who protrude farthest *a tergo*. The yellow races find European noses ridiculously and disagreeably large. Many Negro tribes prefer the blackest-skinned women. In general, each group tends to prefer a slight exaggeration of its own distinctive characters. Darwin accordingly suggested that many racial differences in man owe their origin to sexual selection. His arguments on this subject seem sound. The one serious defect in his treatment is his failure to realize that masculine ornamentation and fine clothes are primarily status symbols concerned with male rivalry, social position, and the class system.

Generally speaking, although Darwin's theory of sexual selection by female choice cannot stand as he originally stated it, although he lumped together

Women's fashions often
have a biological basis,
as with the bustle

several kinds of display with quite different functions—notably threat and
advertisement against actual and potential rivals, and sexual stimulation of
actual and potential mates—and although he omitted to notice the important
subject of mutual display and the formation of emotional bonds, yet he was
perfectly correct in deducing that intra-sexual competition leads to the development of male strength and masculine weapons. In any case, he grasped the
essential point that all striking displays must have some biological meaning and
confer some biological advantage, and the further point that they can only
exert their effect via the sense-organs and exertions of another individual—in
technical jargon they are allaesthetic characters.

Adornment sometimes serves merely to exaggerate feminine distinctiveness, as with the giraffe-necked women of Burma

Thus the second part of *The Descent of Man*, as well as providing us, like all Darwin's major works, with an amazing treasury of strange and interesting facts, has been the starting-point for a whole series of new observations and experiments, which have abundantly proved that displays do play an essential part in promoting successful mating between members of the same species, and also, by their distinctiveness, in preventing mating between members of different species.

But perhaps the most important point is that Darwin found it necessary to distinguish two distinct kinds of selection. Only recently have we been discovering how essential this is, though our categories are rather different. Instead of distinguishing natural and sexual selection, today we regard all selection as natural, but within it we distinguish survival selection and reproductive selection. Survival selection is concerned with characters which help the individual to survive more successfully in the struggle for existence: because these are largely inherited; survival selection will have an evolutionary effect in improving the genetic make-up of the organism in relation to the conditions of its life. Reproductive selection, on the other hand, is concerned with characters which enable the individual to reproduce more successfully than others, characters such as capacity to mate, clutch and litter size, parental care, and so forth.

One school of geneticists insist on defining biological fitness entirely in terms of success in having more offspring than other individuals or groups. This leads to the paradox, or should we rather say the absurdity, of maintaining that rapidly reproducing human stocks are 'fitter', even if their other characters, such as strength, intelligence, and what in normal parlance is called physical fitness are below the average and far below the best.

In *The Descent of Man* Darwin actually paid great attention to the gradual evolution of the mental powers of the higher animals, including man. He had originally intended to write a whole chapter on the emotions and their expression, but soon perceived that the subject merited a separate volume to itself. Accordingly in *The Descent* he devotes a mere four pages to the subject, stressing the obvious fact that higher animals and man share the same basic emotions, and giving examples to show that some mammals at least are animated by more complex emotions such as shame, dislike of being laughed at, desire for deliberate revenge, and even a sense of humour.

'Expression of the Emotions'

Horror and agony:
an illustration from Darwin's
*The Expression of the Emotions
in Man and Animals*

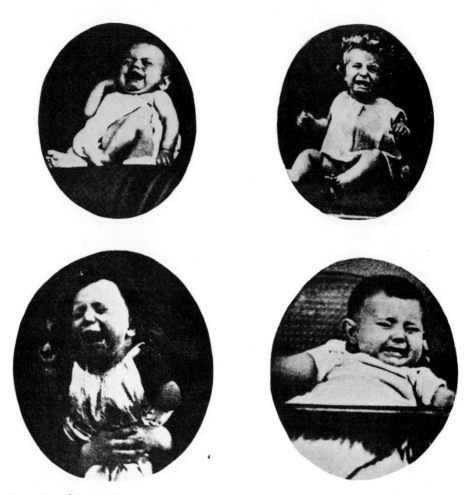

Expression of the emotions: Darwin noted with scientific detachment the wholehearted abandon of a crying baby

Darwin's interest in the subject was of long standing. In one of his earliest notebooks he wrote, 'A capital passage might be made from comparison of man with expression of monkey when offended, who loves, who fears, who is curious etc. etc. etc.' His first child was born late in 1839; as Darwin writes in his *Autobiography*, 'I at once commenced to make notes on the first dawn of the various expressions which he exhibited, for I felt convinced, even at this early period, that the most complex and fine shades of expression must have had a gradual and natural origin'—the first postulate of his theory of evolution.

In the following year he read Sir Charles Bell's celebrated work on the *Anatomy of Expression*, which 'greatly increased the interest which I felt in the subject, though I could not at all agree with his belief that various muscles had been specially created for the sake of expression in man'; for this contradicted Darwin's firm conviction that man was descended from lower animals by gradual transformation. Accordingly from that time on he set himself to collect facts on the subject, which served as the raw material out of which he fashioned his 400-page book *The Expression of the Emotions in Man and Animals*, published in November 1872. On the day of publication 5,267 copies were sold—a remarkable tribute to Darwin's reputation, to his skill in amassing and marshalling relevant facts, and to the book's extraordinary interest as the first serious attempt to apply evolutionary principles to the subject.

In it, Darwin deals with the expression of the entire range of emotional states —joy and affection, pain and anger, fear and terror, grief and laughter, love and devotion, attention and curiosity—including complex emotions or sentiments like hatred, jealousy, sulkiness, disgust, astonishment, admiration, and shame. On many of these, Darwin's own dog Bob provided excellent illustrative material.

Threat: as Darwin pointed out the arched back, the bristling fur, and the snarling mouth help the frightened but hostile cat to appear more formidable

Besides dogs and their wild relatives, he devotes especial attention to the emotional expressions of cats, horses, monkeys, and apes; but he also cites facts concerning cattle and sheep (which he finds on the whole very inexpressive), deer, elephants (which will weep with grief), rabbits, porcupines, hyenas, wild boars, and kangaroos, together with a few birds, reptiles, and amphibians. He concludes that modes of expression are innate in animals, and vary markedly from species to species; on this, he cites the interesting observation that some monkeys when pleased draw back the corners of their mouth so as to expose their teeth—an expression which, as Darwin says, 'would never be recognized by a stranger as one of pleasure'.

As regards man, he paid special attention to infants, because the expression of their emotions is uninhibited, and clearly innate. He was especially concerned to study the insane, 'as they are liable to the strongest passions, and give uncontrolled vent to them'. Here he was much helped by Dr Crichton Browne, who was in charge of a large asylum and provided Darwin with copious notes

In his own dog, Bob, Darwin noted the rigid straight lines of hostile threat, the relaxed curves of submissive affection

Baboon (*Cynopithecus niger*)
expressing pleasure
at being caressed

and some remarkable photographs. He also enlisted the co-operation of a French medical man, Dr Duchenne, who was able to produce the appearance of various emotions by faradic stimulation of the muscles concerned in their expression.

In order to test how far the expression of the emotions in man is innate and similar in different races, and how far it has to be learnt, like language, Darwin circulated a questionnaire comprising sixteen pertinent questions to a number of people in different countries, including missionaries to primitive peoples. From their answers he was able to draw the conclusion (with which most modern anthropologists would agree) that the expressions of simpler or more basic emotions like rage and pleasure, sorrow and disgust, and actions like shrugging the shoulders as a sign of incapacity to cope with a situation or raising and opening the hands as an expression of wonder are innate or at least primarily and mainly determined by heredity; whereas the expression of more elaborate emotions and states of mind like assent or disagreement, reverence or supplication, and actions like kissing are largely determined by the individual's social background and have to be consciously learnt or more often unconsciously acquired.

Ritualized (displacement) preening in the male display actions of various species of duck

Darwin of course stressed the fundamental fact, whose implications have been worked out in detail by modern ethologists like Lorenz and Tinbergen, that the physical expression of emotion provides an important means of communication both for animals and for men. Frequently it represents what today is called an intention-movement, a preparation for some type of action: thus baring and gnashing the teeth express preparation for violent attack or defence, and let other animals know what to expect.

However, he also noted how certain of our more emotional states, like that of puzzlement, are expressed in apparently irrelevant actions like scratching our heads. Modern field studies have shown that similarly irrelevant actions are common in animals—for instance half-hearted preening in the middle of birds' courtship-displays. Such displacement-activities, as they are now called, seem to result from conflict situations (in bird display, conflict between sexual attraction, hostility, and fear) in which none of the conflicting drives gains the upper hand, and the nervous tension can only be released through some other channel.

The astonishing display of
the male Argus pheasant:
illustration from
The Descent of Man

Darwin also drew attention to the exaggerated character of various expressions of emotion, as seen in the expansion of the strikingly patterned hood and the swaying motions of angry cobras; in the imposing attitude of hostile swans with arched wings and violent propulsion with both feet simultaneously; or in the unbelievable elaboration and strangeness of the male Argus pheasant's sexual display. Such exaggeration and formalization certainly make the actions more effective as a means of influencing the behaviour of other animals, whether by intimidating rivals or enemies or by stimulating mates. And it is now clear

C. K. Sprengel, in his famous book, *Nature's Secret Revealed*, described the role of insects in pollination, and decorated the title-page with engravings of insects and flowers

that this psychological enhancement of expression by ritualization, as we now call it, has been brought about by natural selection because of the biological advantages it incurs.

Modern research has of course enormously enlarged our knowledge and clarified our ideas about emotions and their expression. But it remains true that *The Expression of the Emotions* was the first attempt to treat the subject from a purely naturalistic and evolutionary angle, and that it succeeded in stimulating widespread interest and research among scientists, both biologists and human psychologists. Indeed, it marked the birth of the new science of ethology, which is today playing a vital role in helping our quarrelsome psychological sects— psychoanalysts, behaviourists, learning theorists, clinical psychiatrists, experimental psychologists, and the rest—to come together and, one hopes, to achieve a much-needed synthesis.

Adaptation in plants   Darwin himself said that it always gave him pleasure to exalt the vegetable kingdom. His six botanical books all did this, partly by revealing unexpected capacities in plants, such as digestion of animal food, and highly developed

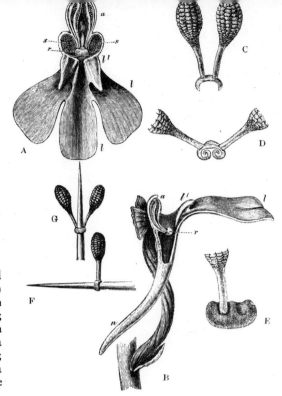

The British pyramidal orchid
(*Orchis pyramidalis*)
A, front view; B, side view, with
most sepals and petals removed;
C, the two pollinia *in situ*, on
their sticky disk; D, the pollinia
diverging after exposure to air;
F, G, as D and E, but pollinia
removed by means of a needle

powers of movement, but mainly by demonstrating the almost incredible adaptations that they exhibit.

Two of the books, however, were concerned primarily with finding the gradual steps by which the well-developed power of movement shown by many unrelated groups of plants must, according to Darwin's principle, have evolved, while the main aim of three others was to demonstrate the over-riding importance of cross-fertilization in nature.

Most flowering plants are hermaphrodite, with both male and female organs present in the same flower. Up to the 1860s the accepted view was that this served to ensure self-fertilization. Darwin, however, had long had doubts on the subject: already in his notebook for 1837 he had pointed out that exclusive self-pollination would mean the existence of innumerable separate lines of descent within a species, each liable to vary independently of the rest, and that a considerable degree of cross-pollination was necessary for a species to share a common store of hereditary variations.

Furthermore, though Sprengel in his famous book of 1793, *Das entdeckte Geheimnis der Natur* ('Nature's Secret Revealed') had shown that bees and other insects were concerned in pollination, neither he nor anyone else had pointed out the basic difference between pollinating the same flower or other flowers on the same plant, and pollinating those of another plant.

The early spider orchid and other species of *Ophrys* puzzled Darwin by the absence of nectar. We now know that they attract male insects by resembling insect females

In 1856 Darwin had written to Hooker, pointing out a statistical fact he had dug out for himself, that more trees of all kinds are one-sexed, with each individual bearing only male or only female flowers, than herbaceous plants. This he rightly ascribed to the huge numbers of separate flowers on each tree, which would make self-pollination, whether by wind or insects, very much more likely. If cross-fertilization confers an advantage, this prevalent uni-sexuality of trees constitutes an adaptation. Darwin then set himself to discover other adaptations which demonstrably necessitated or favoured cross-pollination.

Orchids were abundant near Down, and served as his first objects of study. Darwin showed that insects visited orchid flowers to obtain nectar from their long spurs, and that in the process the club-shaped pollen-masses characteristic of orchids become attached to the insect's proboscis by means of special sticky disks, are pulled out of their sheaths, and, when dried by exposure to the air, move down and apart so that when the insect visits another flower they leave some of their pollen on the sticky receptive pads of the female stigma.

Darwin was puzzled by the absence of nectar in orchid genera like *Ophrys*. Only recently has it been shown that these species are pollinated by pseudo-copulation. Male insects visit them because they mistake them for female insects. In their attempts to mate with these false females, the males become coated with pollen and transport it to effect the real fertilization of other flowers. The presence of nectar would not merely be of no advantage, but would dis-tract the insects from performing their adaptive job—adaptive, that is to say, for the plant. Victorian propriety might have been shocked by these facts: certainly Archdeacon Paley would have had to ascribe some curious propen-sities to their Divine Designer.

Darwin then went on to study foreign orchids, and found in them even more astonishing adaptations. One Madagascar orchid had an eleven-inch spur with nectar in its lower tip. Entomologists denied that any insect could have a proboscis as long as this; but not long afterwards a hawk-moth was discovered in Madagascar with a proboscis of just this length.

Another tropical orchid genus, *Coryanthes*, has a lip transformed into a miniature bucket, which is filled by drops of fluid from two areas of secretory tissue above it. Still farther up are two ridges whose fleshy substance is much appreciated by bumble-bees. Some of the bumble-bees tumble into the bucket: climbing out by the only firm path available up its slippery surface, they get pollen-masses stuck to their backs, and these will fertilize other flowers.

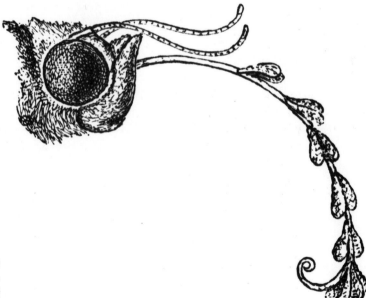

Head and proboscis of the
British moth *Acontia luctuosa*,
with seven pairs of pollen-masses
of the pyramidal orchid attached

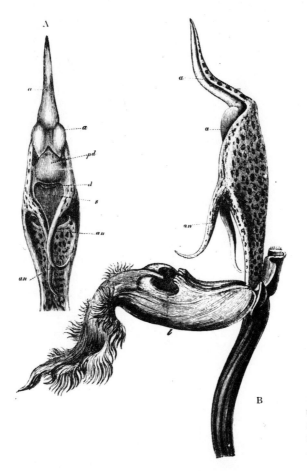

Catasetum saccatum, an orchid
that fascinated Darwin by its
ingenious method of catapulting
its pollen-masses on to an
invading bee's back

But perhaps the most extraordinary adaptation is that of *Catasetum* (which,
by the way, has separate male and female flowers). The pollen-masses of the
male flowers are held under tension: visiting bees inevitably touch a special
trigger, which releases the tension and sets the pollen-mass free to turn a somer-
sault in the air and land with its adhesive disk plump on the bee's back.

As Darwin wrote with his customary careful phrasing, 'the more I study
nature, the more I become impressed that the contrivances and beautiful adaptations through each part occasionally varying in a slight degree, but in many
ways . . . transcend in an incomparable manner the contrivances and adaptations
which the most fertile imagination of man could invent.' Three-quarters
of a century later, R. A. Fisher put the point in the pithy paradox that
natural selection is a mechanism for generating an extremely high degree of
improbability.

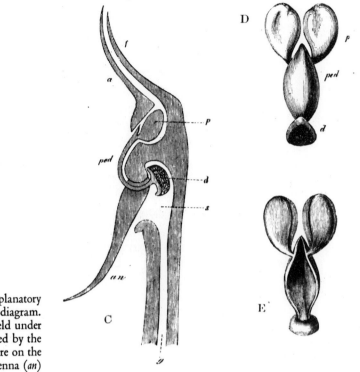

C. *saccatum*: explanatory diagram. The pollen-masses, held under tension, are released by the slightest pressure on the projecting antenna (*an*)

Darwin next turned his attention to the common primrose. Primroses, like cowslips and most other primulas, exist in two forms differing in the structure of their flowers: one called *pin-eyed* because the long style, capped with a pin-head stigma, reaches to the top of the corolla tube, with the stamens half-way down; the other called *thrum-eyed*, with stamens and stigma in reverse positions. Up till Darwin's time, this fact had usually been dismissed as of no particular significance. He, however, showed first that the two types were hereditary; second, that plants fertilized by pollen from the opposite form set much more seed than those fertilized by their own pollen or the pollen from another flower of the same form; and third, that the proboscises of the bees that visited primroses were nicely adapted to achieve the more favourable result.

Darwin recorded in his *Autobiography* that of all of what he called his 'little discoveries', this gave him the greatest satisfaction. Indeed, it was a remarkable piece of pioneering work and though his facts and conclusions were at first disbelieved, even by some professional botanists, they have been fully confirmed, and in modern times their elaborate genetic basis has been thoroughly analysed.

'Different Forms of Flowers'

After publishing a scientific paper on Primula in 1862, he went on to demonstrate the same type of adaptation favouring cross-fertilization in another British plant, the purple loosestrife, *Lythrum salicaria*: here, however, affairs are more complicated, there being three alternative forms differing in lengths of styles and stamens. In 1876 he brought out a book on *Different Forms of Flowers in Plants of the Same Species*.

He also studied other adaptations for securing cross-pollination, and in 1875 published a comprehensive work on the subject, entitled *Effects of Cross- and Self-fertilization in the Vegetable Kingdom*. This convincingly demonstrated that there must be some general biological value in cross-fertilization, and opened the door to modern genetic studies of such problems as heterosis or hybrid vigour, and its practical results in the creation of the new and profitable hybrid grain industry, as well as to important ideas about the evolution of breeding-systems in general.

As a result of these studies, Darwin came to grasp 'how a flower and a bee might slowly become . . . modified and adapted to each other in the most perfect manner', and indeed how, over the last eighty million years or so, flower-visiting insects and flowering plants have evolved in mutual interaction, achieving a symbiosis beneficial to both parties. Sometimes the relation is very specialized: only one species of moth can fertilize the long-spurred Madagascar orchid, only bumble-bees can fertilize red clover.

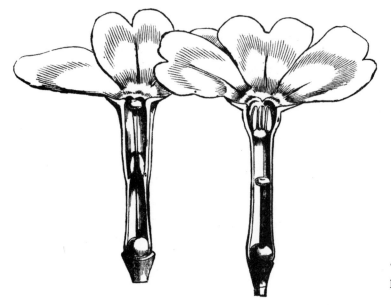

The two flower forms of the primrose (*Primula vulgaris*): (*left*), pin-eyed; (*right*), thrum-eyed

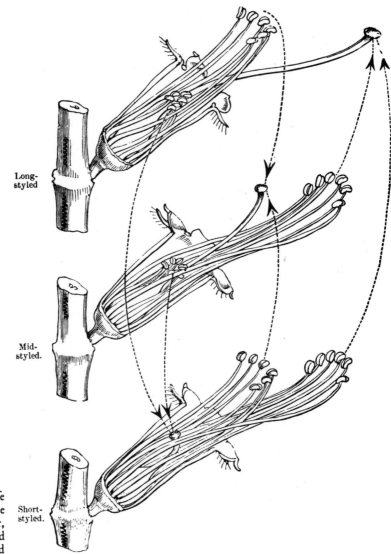

Long-
styled

Mid-
styled.

Purple loosestrife
(*Lythrum salicaria*) has three
different forms of flower,
long-styled, mid-styled, and
short-styled

Short-
styled.

This last fact led Darwin on to one of his classic chains of reasoning—concerning the connexion between cats and clover. The survival of red clover depends on bumble-bees; the number of bumble-bees depends on the number of field-mice, which destroy bumble-bees' nests; and the number of field-mice depends on the number of cats prowling the hedgerows. A later writer extended the ecological chain to include old maids, who are proverbially fond of keeping cats.

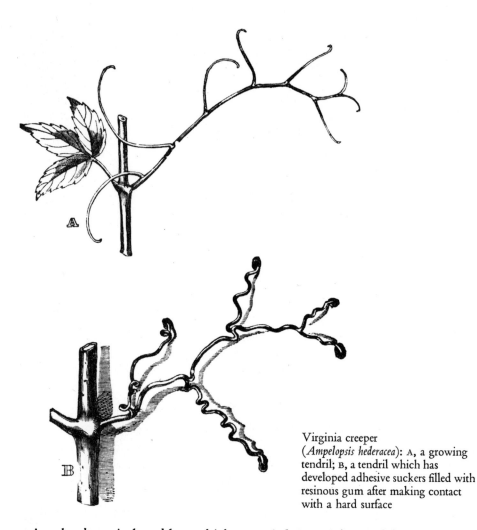

Virginia creeper
(*Ampelopsis hederacea*): A, a growing
tendril; B, a tendril which has
developed adhesive suckers filled with
resinous gum after making contact
with a hard surface

Climbing plants   Another botanical problem which occupied Darwin's mind for many years
was the climbing capacity of plants. This exists in many independent groups
and in many forms. Some plants twine left-handedly, others right-handedly;
some climb by hooks, others by tendrils, sometimes with suckers at their tips.
Here again Darwin was able to demonstrate the existence of intermediate stages
in the development of many remarkable adaptations. He first published his
results in a long scientific paper in 1865, which he expanded into a book ten
years later.

In the interim, aided by his son Frank, he had carried out many observations
and experiments on these and other types of movement in plants, including the
movements of pistils and stamens, of root tips, of shoots bending towards or

Charles Darwin on the veranda at Down House

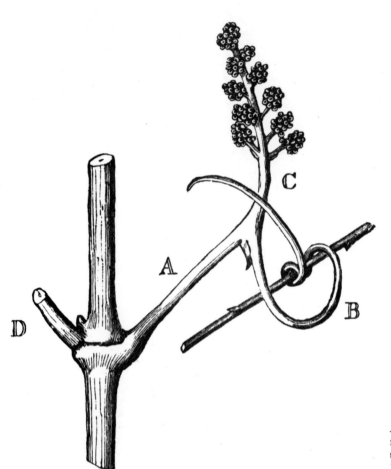

A vine tendril (B) coiled
round a branch to support
the budding flower shoot (C).
Drawn by Darwin's son George

away from light. In this field, too, Darwin made some important new discoveries. Thus he found that the bending of a growing shoot towards the light
falling on one side of the tip is due to the more rapid growth of the opposite side
of the shoot, but at a spot some distance from the tip. And this extra growth
takes place even when the growing part is shielded from all light. This means
that something must travel or be conducted from the site of the stimulus (light)
to the site of the effect (differential growth). Here again Darwin's results were
scornfully rejected by other workers in the field, even by such an eminent
botanist as Julius von Sachs; but they were abundantly confirmed, and indeed
served as the starting-point for a whole series of further experiments which have
led to what is virtually a new science—the science of growth-hormones and
their manifold effects in all sorts of plants.

Darwin's walking-stick, with spiral grooves made by a climbing plant

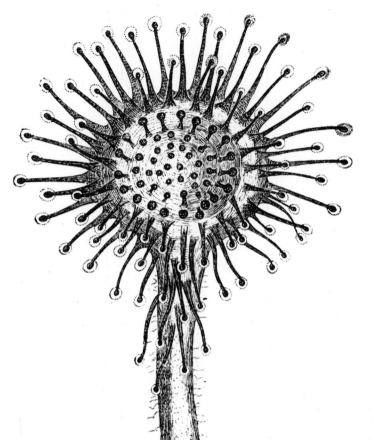

Sundew leaf
(*Drosera rotundifolia*)
with tentacles
extended

There remains the strange phenomenon of carnivorous plants. Already in 1860, when on holiday in Sussex after preparing the second edition of *The Origin*, Darwin's naturalist eye was struck by the number of tiny insects trapped by the peculiar leaves of that common bog plant, the sundew, *Drosera rotundi-folia*: he counted thirty-one captured by twelve plants. During the next fifteen years, he, at first alone but later aided by Frank, performed a fantastic range of experiments on this and other insect-trapping plants, which he summarized in a fascinating book entitled simply *Insectivorous Plants*. He proved that any small object touching the sticky knob at the end of one of a sundew leaf's tentacles acted as a stimulus, causing it and all the other tentacles to bend and close towards the centre of the leaf, and to secrete a juice capable of digesting most types of animal flesh. As with the effects of light on plant shoots, something is transmitted (through the cells of the leaf, not through its woody vessels) which stimulates the tentacles to bend inwards and to secrete digestive fluid.

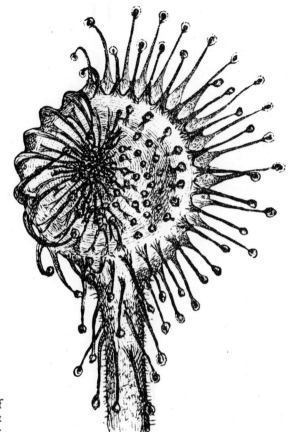

Sundew leaf
with tentacles bent
over a scrap of meat

The delicacy of the response amazed Darwin, and continues to amaze us today. A fragment of woman's hair weighing less than a millionth of a gram would set the mechanism off, proving that *Drosera* tentacles were far more responsive than Darwin's own tongue and seventy-eight times as sensitive as the most delicate chemical balance of his day.

The soluble products of the digested insects are absorbed into the tissue of the plant; this makes up for the paucity of nitrogen in the poor boggy soils that it and other insectivorous plants inhabit. When various European botanists asserted that this capacity to digest proteins was of no biological value, Darwin's son Frank, later Professor Francis Darwin, grew two lots of *Drosera*, one fed with meat, the other not fed. He found that the meat-fed plants produced more and bigger leaves, flower stalks and seed capsules. The capacity to catch and digest animal prey is thus undoubtedly a very beautiful and elaborate adaptation to a particular type of habitat.

Darwin is sometimes dismissed by modern laboratory biologists as merely a naturalist, devoted only to the amassing of innumerable facts of observation. A naturalist he certainly was; but in his botanical studies he revealed himself as a great experimentalist, and paved the way for that combination of field study and laboratory experiment that is proving so fruitful in present-day biology.

Earthworms and history Darwin's last book was published on 10 October 1881. It was on earthworms and, like all his other books, grew out of an idea which had long previously germinated in his mind. In this case the latent period was forty-four years. Soon after his return from the *Beagle* voyage, his interest was aroused by his uncle Josiah Wedgwood's remarking on the amount of soil brought up by the worms on the lawn at Maer; within a year's time he read a paper before the Geological Society concluding that worms could speedily bury all surface objects. How pleased he would have been to learn that in 1964 an increase in worm population had been recommended to improve the race-course at Ascot!

The Worm Stone,
Down House

The drawing-room, Down House. Earthworms placed in a pot on the piano reacted to a deep bass note

Twenty-two years later, a critic in the *Gardeners' Chronicle*, attacking Darwin's views, wrote that worms, because of their weakness and small size, were wholly incapable of such a 'stupendous feat'. This revealed the writer's inability to grasp one of the central postulates of all Darwin's work—the postulate that, given enough time, small and gradual causes can produce large and radical effects—and provoked him to set about collecting more evidence on the subject. He counted the number of worm-tracks on his walks, put up a special 'worm stone' in the lawn at Down and measured the rate at which it sank, made a careful study of earthworms' anatomy, physiology, and habits, watched and experimented on worms in pots he brought into his study, and made midnight excursions on to the lawn to study the effects of vibration and light on the creatures; when he blew a whistle or played a bassoon to them, they made no response, but a deep bass note on the piano on which a pot of worms was placed at once sent them into their burrows, presumably because of the mechanical vibrations it caused.

Stonehenge: Darwin showed that earthworms had begun to bury stones that had fallen on the turf

He found that in thirty years, worms had buried every flint on a once very stony field; in spite of ill-health he travelled to Stonehenge and showed that worms had caused the great monoliths to settle into the earth; and he finally discovered that in the space of well under 2,000 years worms had buried the tile floor of a Roman villa so deep below the surface of a ploughed field that its presence had never been suspected. He was able to calculate that on every acre of the chalk hills near Down, worms brought up eighteen tons of earth annually, and that the burying of stones on the surface went on at the rate of about a quarter of an inch every year—of course only down to the depth of the earthworms' burrows, which range from twelve to twenty inches in different soils. Thus every few years the entire soil of the English countryside is subjected to a natural form of cultivation by being triturated, mixed, and enriched in its passage through the bodies of earthworms.

Charles Darwin: the last photograph

After twelve years, he was ready to publish. On 1 May 1881, he wrote in his *Autobiography* that he had just sent to the printers the MS. of 'my little book on the Formation of Vegetable Mould through the Action of Worms. This is a subject of but small importance; and I know not whether it will interest any readers.' In point of fact, it interested a great many: 8,500 copies were sold in just over three years, and it has been frequently reprinted since.

The book is valuable as an example of Darwin's methods of tackling biological problems, and as a beautiful and simple demonstration of his central thesis that small, long-continued causes can produce great results. It is also of historical importance as the first quantitative ecological study of an animal's role in nature. Indeed, it may properly be claimed that through it Darwin became one of the founding fathers of ecology, that focal study which is becoming so vitally important to our overcrowded globe.

Conclusion   In the winter of 1881–1882 Darwin's heart began to give serious trouble: after one attack he had difficulty in making his way back on his customary Sandwalk. After his seventy-third birthday, on 12 February 1882, he wrote to a friend, 'my course is nearly run'. Indeed it was: after a short final illness, Darwin died of a severe heart attack on 19 April. Yet in the six months between the publication of the earthworm book and his death, he published six scientific communications, on such diverse subjects as the cuckoo-like brood-parasitism of cowbirds, the action of ammonium carbonate on plants, the dispersal of freshwater bivalve molluscs, and the effects of sexual selection on Syrian street-dogs. What an astonishing man!

As the result of a letter addressed to the Dean of Westminster by twenty M.P.s, Darwin was accorded the honour of burial in Westminster Abbey. His pall-bearers included the President of the Royal Society; Darwin's three closest scientific friends, who were also the three leading British biologists, Huxley, Hooker, and Wallace; the liberal churchman Canon Farrar; an earl and two dukes; and Robert Lowell, the American Minister.

And so the two greatest scientists that England has produced came to lie side by side in the Abbey—Newton, who banished miracles from the physical world and reduced God to the role of a cosmic designer who on the day of creation had brought the clockwork mechanism of the universe into being to tick away according to the inevitable laws of its nature; and Darwin, who banished not only miracles but also creation and design from the world of life, robbed God of his role of creator of man, and man of his divine origin. This seems at first only an ironic tribute to the power of science to destroy old dogmas and illusions; but it is also a tribute to new hopes and new achievements. Newton opened the door to a rational understanding of physical nature and to its technological control; Darwin opened the door to a rational understanding

MAN·IS·BVT·A·WORM·

'Man is but a Worm'—but an evolved worm: *Punch* cartoon

of man and his place and role in nature, and to the possibility of improving the human condition.

What strikes one most forcibly about Darwin's career is the combined depth and range of his achievements during the fifty years of his scientific activity. By pursuing the basic idea of evolution by natural selection to the fullest possible extent, he changed the whole framework of human thought, substituting a dynamic and progressive vision of existence for the traditional view, with its uneasy combination of the static and the apocalyptic. In the process he made important discoveries in geology, botany, palaeontology, genetics, reproduction, behaviour, and general natural history; virtually created the new sciences of

The memorial tablets to Wallace and Darwin, Westminster Abbey

ecology and ethology; laid the foundations for a scientific taxonomy, and prepared the way for a rational anthropology.

He sat quietly at Down like a benevolent spider at the centre of a world-wide web of scientific communication, by means of which he amassed a prodigious store of knowledge in all the sciences of earth, life, and man. But the knowledge was not merely amassed for its own sake, nor to satisfy his collector's instinct: it was always collected with a definite end in view—to test some hypothesis or buttress some theoretical principle. With the aid of that knowledge and those principles, he was able to follow up the implications of his ideas to their limit, with the unusual result that his books can still be read with profit by professional biologists as well as by the lay public a hundred years after they were written.

What strikes one most forcibly about Darwin as a man is his passion for truth, his devotion to his self-appointed task, his extraordinary modesty, his hatred of cruelty and injustice, and his essential goodness.

Quite apart from his contributions to science and human understanding, Darwin's career stands as a shining encouragement to those who fail to fit into the correct academic mould in our educational system in their youth. His particular powers had little opportunity of showing themselves till late in his life. He proved that curiosity and initiative, scrupulous honesty and wide-ranging interest are sufficient for success and indeed essential for the conquest of new horizons.

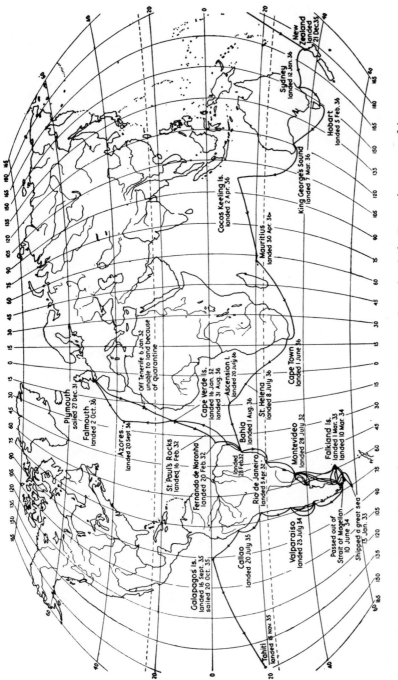

The voyage of the *Beagle*, 1831–1836. From Sir Gavin de Beer's *Charles Darwin*, by courtesy of the author and Thomas Nelson and Sons Ltd

New Zealand landed 21 Dec. 35

Sydney landed 12 Jan. 36

Hobart landed 5 Feb. 36

King George's Sound landed 7 Mar. 36

Cocos Keeling Is. landed 2 Apr. 36

Mauritius landed 30 Apr. 36

Cape Town landed 1 June 36

St. Helena landed 8 July 36

Ascension I. landed 20 July 36

Cape Verde Is. landed 16 Jan. 32 landed 31 Aug. 36

Off Tenerife 6 Jan. 32 unable to land because of quarantine

Plymouth sailed 27 Dec. 31

Falmouth landed 2 Oct. 36

Azores landed 20 Sept 36

St. Paul's Rocks landed 16 Feb. 32

Fernando de Noronha landed 20 Feb. 32

Bahia landed 28 Feb. 32

Rio de Janeiro landed 5 Apr. 32

Montevideo landed 28 July 32

Falkland Is. landed 1 Mar. 33 landed 10 Mar. 34

Valparaiso landed 23 July 34

Callao landed 20 July 35

Galapagos Is. landed 16 Sept. 35 sailed 20 Oct. 35

Passed out of Strait of Magellan 10 June 34

Shipped a great sea 13 Jan. 33

Tahiti landed 16 Nov. 35

ACKNOWLEDGMENT

The authors make grateful acknowledgment to Lady Barlow, Darwin's grand-daughter, who, apart from showing them Darwin manuscripts held by her, has given them the benefit of her views on many aspects of her grandfather's life and work; also to Professor A. W. Woodruff of the London School of Tropical Medicine, who has given them much information on the pathology of Chagas' disease whilst, at the same time, thinking it unlikely that Darwin's illness resulted from it.

1809 12 February. Born at Shrewsbury, the son of Dr Robert Waring Darwin, 'the largest man whom I ever saw'

1817 Goes to the Rev. G. Case's school as a day-boy

1818 Enters Shrewsbury School, under Dr Butler's headmastership. 'Nothing could have been worse for the development of my mind'

1825 Enters Edinburgh University to study medicine. Shows interest in natural history, and attends lectures on geology, but decides medicine is not for him. His father sends him to Cambridge to read divinity

1827 15 October. Admitted to Christ's College

1831 26 April. Receives his B.A. degree, tenth in the list of pass degrees
24 August. The Rev. J. S. Henslow, Professor of Botany, tells him of Captain FitzRoy's offer of a berth in the *Beagle*. His father's opposition overcome by Josiah Wedgwood, he sails with the *Beagle* from Devonport two days after Christmas

1832 16 January. Lands 'for first time on a tropical shore' (Cape Verde Islands). 'It has been for me a glorious day'
28 February. *Beagle* anchors at Bahia, Brazil. 'The land is a chaos of delight'

1833 3 January. *Beagle* reaches Tierra del Fuego and returns Jemmy Button, York Minster, and Fuegia Basket to their native land

1834 9 June. *Beagle* rounds Cape Horn and enters the Pacific. Darwin is ill for a month in the autumn, with an un-identified illness

1835 26 March. Severely bitten by Benchuca bug (*Triatoma infestans*). This may have resulted in a latent infection of Chagas' disease, manifesting itself later in years of ill-health
September. *Beagle* visits the Galápagos Islands, where divergent species of finch cause first glimmerings of theory of evolutionary transformation

1836 2 October. *Beagle* drops anchor at Falmouth, 'five years and two days' since Darwin left home. After a visit to his family he takes rooms in Cambridge

1837 Moves to 36 Great Marlborough Street, London, to sort out his collections and arrange for the writing of his report
July. He starts his first notebook on trans-mutation of species

1838 Becomes Secretary of the Geological Society. Visits Glen Roy, and writes paper on the 'parallel roads'
October. He reads 'for amusement Malthus on population', and realizes that natural selection must be the mechanism that tends to the preservation of favourable variations
11 November. He proposes to his cousin Emma Wedgwood. 'The day of days'

1839 1 January. Moves in to 12 Upper Gower Street, London
29 January. Married at Maer. In the spring, he first meets Joseph Dalton Hooker
August. *Journal of Researches* (Vol. III of FitzRoy's *Narrative of the Surveying Voyages of H.M.S. 'Adventure' and 'Beagle'*) published

1842 May. Writes pencil sketch of 'my Species Theory'. Publication of *The Structure and Distribution of Coral Reefs*
September. The Darwins move to Down House, Kent

1844 July to September. Writes fuller version of species theory

1846 1 October. Begins work on Cirripedes (barnacles). *Geological Observations on South America* published in December

1854 Having completed work on barnacles (published in 2 vols., 1851 and 1854), 'finished packing up all my Cirripedes. Began sorting notes for Species Theory'

1856 14 May. Urged on by Hooker and Lyell, he begins writing 'Species Sketch'
16 December. Finishes Chapter 3

1857 Eight chapters finished by the end of September

1858 18 June. Receives letter from Alfred Russel Wallace containing complete outline of evolutionary theory based on natural selection. Forwards it to Sir Charles Lyell: 'your words have come true with a vengeance—that I should be forestalled'
1 July. Joint paper with Wallace read to the Linnaean Society
28 July. Begins to write 'Abstract of Species book', i.e. *The Origin of Species*

1859 24 November. *The Origin of Species* published. First edition, 1,250 copies, sold out the same day

1860 7 January. *The Origin of Species*, 2nd ed. (3,000 copies)
28 June. British Association meeting at Oxford; the Wilberforce-Huxley debate

1861 30 April. *The Origin of Species*, 3rd ed. (2,000 copies)

1862 15 May. Publication of book *On the Various Contrivances by which British and Foreign Orchids are Fertilized by Insects*

1864 30 November. Awarded the Copley Medal of the Royal Society

1866 June. *The Origin of Species*, 4th ed. (1,250 copies)

1868 30 January. Publication of *The Variation of Animals and Plants Under Domestication*. Reprinted within a month

1869 7 August. *The Origin of Species*, 5th ed. (2,000 copies)

1871 24 February. Publication of *The Descent of Man, and Selection in Relation to Sex*. 'Man in his arrogance thinks himself a great work worthy the interposition of a deity. More humble and I believe truer to consider him created from animals'

1872 19 February. *The Origin of Species*, 6th ed. (3,000 copies)
26 November. *The Expression of the Emotions in Man and Animals* published

1875 2 July. Publication of *Insectivorous Plants*
September. Publication of book *On the Movements and Habits of Climbing Plants*

1876 May–June. Wrote his autobiographical sketch, published in 1887 by his son Francis as part of *The Life and Letters of Charles Darwin*
10 November. Publication of *Effects of Cross- and Self-fertilization in the Vegetable Kingdom*

1880 6 November. Publication of *The Power of Movement in Plants*

1881 10 October. Publication of 'my little book on the Formation of Vegetable Mould through the Action of Worms'

1882 19 April. He dies at Down House after a heart attack, in his seventy-fourth year
26 April. Buried in Westminster Abbey, beside Sir Isaac Newton

Pictures from the Down House Collection are reproduced by courtesy of the President, Royal College of Surgeons of England

Frontispiece. DARWIN AT THE AGE OF TWENTY-NINE. Drawing by T. F. Maguire. *Radio Times Hulton Picture Library*

Page

5 SHREWSBURY FROM COTON HILL. This early-nineteenth-century engraving (by Capone after Browne) shows the town as it was when Dr Darwin's son first went to Dr Butler's school. *By courtesy of the Governing Body of Shrewsbury School*

7 THE MOUNT HOUSE, SHREWSBURY, where Darwin was born, and where his father had a successful medical practice. *Down House*

8 ERASMUS DARWIN, Charles's grandfather, could also be called the grandfather of the evolution theory. In his *The Botanic Garden*, which has been described as 'the best bad poem in the English language', he proposed the idea that all living things are descended from a common ancestor. This silhouette shows him playing chess with Erasmus, his second son. *Down House*

9 ROBERT WARING DARWIN, Charles's father. Over six feet tall and weighing twenty-four stone, 'he was the largest man whom I ever saw'. Miniature by an unknown artist. *Down House*

SUSANNAH DARWIN, Charles's mother, and daughter of Josiah Wedgwood I, died when he was eight. Miniature by Peter Paillou, 1792. *By courtesy of Lady Keynes*

CHARLES, AGED SIX, and his younger sister Catherine. Coloured chalk drawing by Sharples. *By courtesy of George Darwin Esq.*

10 A SCHOOLBOY'S DOODLES in a school atlas, proudly preserved by his old school. Darwin's school career was undistinguished, and 'Nothing', he noted in his *Autobiography*, 'could have been worse for the development of my mind than Dr Butler's school.' *By courtesy of the Governing Body of Shrewsbury School*

11 THE OLD SCHOOLS, Shrewsbury. Founded by Edward VI in 1552, the School was moved from this building (now the Borough Library) to its present site in 1882. *By courtesy of the Governing Body of Shrewsbury School*

13 ERASMUS ALVEY DARWIN, Charles's elder brother. Erasmus studied medicine at Edinburgh at the same time as Charles, and, like him, disappointed Dr Darwin by giving it up. Portrait by George Richmond, 1850. *Down House*

14 THE GATEWAY OF CHRIST'S COLLEGE, CAMBRIDGE. Charles came into residence on 15 October 1827, to read divinity. *Crown copyright reserved. By permission of the Controller, H.M. Stationery Office*

15 DARWIN'S ROOMS were over the doorway to G staircase, Front Court. His time, he wrote later, was wasted as far as study was concerned, and he got involved with 'some dissipated low-minded young men'. *Photograph Stephen England, by courtesy of the Master and Fellows of Christ's College*

16 ADAM SEDGWICK (1785–1873), Professor of Geology at Cambridge University. *Radio Times Hulton Picture Library*

17 REV. JOHN STEVENS HENSLOW (1796–1861), Professor of Botany. Only thirteen years older than Darwin, he befriended the young man, saw that he was more suited for a naturalist than a parson, and recommended him to Captain FitzRoy of the *Beagle*. *Radio Times Hulton Picture Library*

18 'UNCLE JOS'—Josiah Wedgwood II (1769–1843)—was the son of the founder of the Wedgwood pottery firm. His sister married Charles's father, and his daughter married Charles. His home at Maer was like a second home to Charles in his boyhood. Portrait by William Owen. *By courtesy of Josiah Wedgwood and Sons Ltd*

19 THE NEW VICTUALLING OFFICE, Devil's Point, Devonport. From the near-by dockyard the *Beagle* sailed on 27 December 1831. Contemporary print. *By courtesy of J. P. M. Pannell Esq.*

20 ROBERT FITZROY (1805–1865), Captain of the *Beagle*. Portrait painted by Francis Lane after FitzRoy's promotion to Vice-Admiral. *By courtesy of the Royal Naval College, Greenwich (Hospital Collection)*

21 SIDE ELEVATION OF HMS 'BEAGLE', drawn many years after the voyage by Philip Gidley King, whose father commanded Beagle's companion ship, *Adventure*. *By courtesy of Sir Geoffrey Keynes*

MANY HUNDREDS OF COPIES of this cameo by Josiah Wedgwood I (referred to in *The Botanic Garden*, by his friend Erasmus Darwin, as 'the poor fetter'd slave on bended knee/From Britain's sons imploring to be free') were distributed by the master potter as anti-slavery propaganda. Darwin argued passionately with FitzRoy against slavery. Reproduced in *The Botanic Garden*

22 RIO DE JANEIRO, Darwin's base for three months. This drawing, from FitzRoy's *Narrative of the Surveying Voyages of H.M.S. 'Adventure' and 'Beagle'*, is by Augustus Earle. Captain FitzRoy wrote: 'Knowing that no one actively engaged in the surveying duties . . . would have time . . . to make much use of the pencil, I engaged an artist, Mr Augustus Earle.' Ill-health compelled Earle to leave the ship at Montevideo in August 1832

23 BROUGHT FROM TIERRA DEL FUEGO to England by Captain FitzRoy on a previous voyage of the *Beagle*, the three Fuegian natives, Fuegia Basket (*top*), York Minster, and Jemmy Button were given instruction, to quote the Captain, 'in English, and the plainer truths of Christianity, as the first object; the use of common tools, a slight acquaintance with husbandry, gardening, and mechanism as the second'. In London they were received by King William IV and Queen Adelaide in the summer of 1831. Drawing by Captain FitzRoy in the *Narrative*

24 CROSSING THE LINE in the *Beagle* on 17 February 1832. The traditional ceremonies were drawn by Augustus Earle. From FitzRoy's *Narrative*

25 DARWIN FIRST SET FOOT in South America on 28 February 1832 at Bahia. Earle's drawing of the Church of San Salvador is from FitzRoy's *Narrative*

27 CORCOVADO MOUNTAIN, Rio de Janeiro, rises behind the little village of Botofogo, where Darwin lodged. Today the former village is crowded with the villas of wealthy Brazilians. Drawing by Earle from FitzRoy's *Narrative*

28 THE CUSTOM HOUSE, MONTEVIDEO. Here one of the many South American revolutions was taking place when the *Beagle* landed in July 1832. Drawing by Earle from FitzRoy's *Narrative*

29 'TWO STONES COVERED WITH LEATHER and united with a thin plaited thong'—the bolas used by the Argentinians to bring down ostriches and other animals. Nineteenth-century engraving. *Radio Times Hulton Picture Library*

30 TIERRA DEL FUEGO: aerial view of the range now called the Darwin Cordilleras. From Gunter Plüschow's *Silberkondor über Feuerland*. *Radio Times Hulton Picture Library*

31 ONA INDIANS from the interior of Tierra del Fuego. This photograph was taken in the last decade of the nineteenth century; they must have looked very much the same when Darwin saw them in 1832. *Radio Times Hulton Picture Library*

33 ARGENTINIAN GAUCHO. Darwin had these horsemen as his guides on many of his South American expeditions. *Radio Times Hulton Picture Library*

34 ON CHRISTMAS DAY 1833 a party from the *Beagle*, under Mr Chaffers, the master, visited Port Desire Inlet and explored the river at its head. Conrad Martens, the ship's artist, sketched the bivouac. From the *Narrative*

35 THE RELAPSE INTO SAVAGERY of Jemmy Button and his two fellow-Fuegians was swift and complete. Jemmy (*top*) and his wife were drawn by Captain FitzRoy on the *Beagle*'s second visit, in 1834. From the *Narrative*

THE CAPTAIN'S EXPEDITION travelled 245 miles up the Rio Santa Cruz while the *Beagle* was undergoing repairs. At their farthest point, they could see the snow-covered peaks of the Andes. Drawing by Conrad Martens from the *Narrative*

36 THE 'BEAGLE' laid ashore at the mouth of the Rio Santa Cruz, and careened for repairs to her keel. Drawing by Conrad Martens from the *Narrative*

37 ENTERING THE PACIFIC by way of the Straits of Magellan in June 1834, the *Beagle* anchored at the foot of Mount Sarmiento. Watercolour by Conrad Martens. *By courtesy of Commander J. Smyth*

38 IN HIS COLLECTING, Darwin tried to cast his net as widely as possible, not favouring one order over another. The picture shows a case of Coleoptera sent home by him. *Down House*

39 THE GREAT BLACK BUG of the Pampas, Benchuca (*Triatoma infestans*). This creature (actual length about one inch) is known to be a carrier of Chagas' disease, and may have infected Darwin. *By courtesy of Professor A. W. Woodruff*

40 SICK AND EXHAUSTED in the autumn of 1834, as he struggled back from his expedition into the Andes, he still filled his notebooks. From these notebooks (many of which are still kept, tattered and travel-stained, at Down House) he wrote up his account of the voyage, crossing out passages as he made the fair-copy version. *Down House*

41 THE GREAT CHILEAN EARTHQUAKE of 1835 wrecked the town of Concepción while Darwin was there. The ruins of the Cathedral were sketched by Lt Wickham, first officer of the *Beagle*. From FitzRoy's *Narrative*

42 HMS 'BEAGLE' in the Straits of Magellan. The *Beagle* was a ten-gun sloop-brig of 235 tons burthen, 90 feet long and 24 feet 8 inches in the beam. Drawn by R. T. Pritchett for the frontispiece of the 1890 edition of *A Naturalist's Voyage*. *By courtesy of the National Maritime Museum, Greenwich*

43 AMONG THE STRANGE FAUNA of the Galápagos Islands, Darwin would have seen the iguanas, four- to six-foot lizards of prehistoric appearance like this male marine iguana photographed on Narborough Island. *By courtesy of Dr Irenäus Eibl-Eibesfeldt*

44 DERIVED FROM A COMMON ANCESTOR, the finches of the Galápagos Islands, when Darwin saw them, had diverged into fourteen distinct species. (1) *Geospiza magnirostris*, (2) *G. fortis*, (3) *G. parvula*, (4) *Certhidea olivacea* (probably a sub-group of *Geospiza*). The powerful beak of (1) is adapted for seed eating, while (4) is an insect eater; between (1) and (3), Darwin noted, 'there are no less than six species with insensibly graduated beaks'. From *A Naturalist's Voyage*

45 MAORI NATIVES OF NEW ZEALAND, of whom Darwin wrote: 'Ferocity is a striking trait in the countenances of many among the younger men, and it is increased gradually by the savage style in which their faces are disfigured.' Drawing by Captain FitzRoy, from the *Narrative*

46 THE DUCK-BILLED PLATYPUS (*Ornithorhynchus*) which Darwin was fortunate enough to see one evening in Australia, 'playing about the surface of the water'. Drawn by Ferdinand Bauer on the Matthew Flinders expedition (1801). *By courtesy of the Trustees, British Museum (Natural History)*

47 DARWIN'S THEORY of the evolution of coral reefs by subsidence. *Above*: diagram of a mountainous island with fringing reefs (A), and (dotted line) the formation of a barrier reef (A') round a lagoon (C) as a result of subsidence. *Below*: the island with barrier reef (A') and lagoon (C), and (dotted line) the formation of an atoll with surrounding reef (A″) and central lagoon (C') as a result of further subsidence. From *The Structure and Distribution of Coral Reefs*

48 DARWIN'S MICROSCOPE, still to be seen at Down House. This is the instrument he used at home: in the *Beagle* he had a portable microscope of lower power, in a travelling-case. This one, too, is in the Darwin Museum. *Down House*

49 SHREWSBURY AND THE SEVERN. Engraving by C. W. Radcliffe. The Old Shrewsbury School playing-field is in the foreground, with the fives courts in the right foreground. The bridge in the centre is the Welsh Bridge, leading to Frankwell and the Mount, where Darwin's home stood. Darwin used to walk to school along the wall that runs on the near side of the river. *By courtesy of Shrewsbury Borough Library*

50 SIR RICHARD OWEN (1804–1892), a zoologist of more influence than integrity. He accepted the responsibility for cataloguing and describing the fossil mammals among the collections that Darwin brought home from the voyage of the *Beagle*, but after the publication of *The Origin of Species* he became Darwin's bitterest scientific enemy. Oil painting by H. W. Pickersgill, 1845. *By courtesy of the National Portrait Gallery*

51 THE 'PARALLEL ROADS' of Glen Roy. Marking the shore-line of a dammed-up glacial lake, they run clear and level along both sides of this Scottish glen. Interpreting them as marine beaches, formed when the land was much lower, was one of the few egregious errors of Darwin's scientific career, and one which left its mark upon him. *Photograph Stephen England*

52 SIR JOSEPH HOOKER, FRS (1817–1911) was one of Darwin's few scientific confidants and with Lyell was instrumental in persuading him to publish his views on the origin of species. Hooker travelled to the Antarctic as a young man with Sir James Ross, and published Floras of the Antarctic, New Zealand, and Tasmania. He succeeded his father as Director of the Royal Botanic Gardens at Kew. *Radio Times Hulton Picture Library*

53 SIR CHARLES LYELL (1797–1875), the father of modern geology. His *Principles of Geology* (3 vols., 1830–1833) exercised an important influence on Darwin's thought. *Radio Times Hulton Picture Library*

55 THE TASMANIAN WOLF, a marsupial carnivore. Evolution has independently produced wolf-like types both in marsupial and in placental mammals. *By courtesy of the Director, Zoological Society of London*

56 EMMA DARWIN (1808–1896), Charles's wife, and daughter of his uncle Josiah Wedgwood. She bore him ten children, and nursed him devotedly through years of ill-health. After a portrait by George Richmond. *Down House*

57 DARWIN AT THE TIME OF HIS MARRIAGE, aged thirty. Portrait by George Richmond. *Down House*

58 THE DARWINS' FIRST HOME in London, 12 Upper Gower Street. The house was destroyed in an air raid in 1940, and on its site now stands—appropriately—the Biological Sciences block of the University of London. *Whiffin Collection, London County Council Photo Library*

59 AT MAER, NOT FAR FROM DARWIN'S HOME in Shrewsbury, lived Josiah Wedgwood and his attractive daughters. The picture shows St Peter's Church, where Charles and Emma were married on 29 January 1839. In the background, the roof and chimneys of the Wedgwood home. *Thames and Hudson Archives*

60 DOWN HOUSE: the front. Only a few people per year visit this, the world's finest collection of Darwiniana, where the rooms and furniture are kept just as they were when Darwin lived here. *Thames and Hudson Archives*

61 'A VERY GOOD, VERY UGLY HOUSE' was Darwin's description of his last home, Down House at Downe, Kent. View from the back. *Thames and Hudson Archives*

62 DARWIN WITH HIS ELDEST SON, William Erasmus (1839–1914). From a daguerreotype. *By courtesy of George Darwin Esq.*

63 EMMA WITH HER SON LENNY. Major Leonard Darwin (1850–1943) became President of the Eugenics Society. *Down House*

64 THE LAWN AT THE BACK OF DOWN HOUSE was a laboratory for the study of earthworms. In the background is the mulberry tree, still standing under the nursery window. *Thames and Hudson Archives*

65 DARWIN'S NOTES ON HIS HEALTH cover several sheets of foolscap with cryptic abbreviations. How he felt in the daytime, how he slept at night, dizzy spells, bowel movement—everything is there. Was this hypochondria, or his usual patient, obsessive collection of facts? *Down House*

67 THE SANDWALK, or the 'thinking path', as Darwin called it. Here he walked almost every day, for he found that he did some of his most fruitful thinking while taking gentle exercise. *Thames and Hudson Archives*

68 ALFRED RUSSEL WALLACE (1823–1913), drawn from a photograph, 1853. Wallace spent the years 1854–1862 in the Malay archipelago, travelling all over its islands and making extensive notes and vast collections. Here he first began thinking in terms of evolution, and in February 1858, during an attack of fever, he independently hit on the principle of natural selection as the key to evolutionary transformation. He at once wrote out a short statement of his ideas and sent it to Darwin.

69 DARWIN'S STUDY at Down House, until the later part of his life when a new wing was built on to the house. He used the window-seat when he was working with the microscope. *Thames and Hudson Archives*

70 WHEN WALLACE'S LETTER ARRIVED, Darwin, seeing himself forestalled after more than twenty years' work, asked Lyell's and Hooker's advice, and they suggested a joint communication to the Linnean Society. The scene, in its way one of the most dramatic in the history of science, is reconstructed by a Russian artist, Victor Eustaphieff. *By courtesy of the State Darwin Museum, Moscow*

71 'SCRIBBLING IN A VILE HAND whole pages as quickly as I possibly can', Darwin wrote *The Origin of Species* in thirteen months of 1858–1859. Owing to his habit of making notes on the backs of old MSS., very little of *The Origin* MS. is left. *By courtesy of Cambridge University Library*

72 LAST-STAGE LARVAE of the goose barnacle, *Lepas*. Drawn for the *Monograph on the Cirripedia* by George Sowerby the Younger, third generation of a family of artist-naturalists who illustrated a wide range of nineteenth-century natural history

73 THE FIRST EDITION OF *The Origin of Species*, 1,250 copies, was sold out on the day of publication. *Down House*

75 THOMAS HENRY HUXLEY (1825–1895), the greatest zoologist of nineteenth-century England, was bowled over by the simplicity of the concept of natural selection. As soon as he had read *The Origin of Species* he wrote to Darwin, 'I am sharpening up my claws and beak in readiness'—for the battle which was about to be joined. *Photograph by Maull & Polyblank. By courtesy of Sir Julian Huxley*

76 ONE OF THE BITTEREST OPPONENTS OF *The Origin* was Sir Richard Owen—caricatured here in a *Vanity Fair* cartoon. He even criticized it anonymously in the *Edinburgh Review*, buttressing his strictures with approving quotations from 'the famous Professor Owen'. *Down House*

77 SAMUEL WILBERFORCE, Bishop of Oxford (1805–1873), spoke against Darwinism (briefed by Owen) at the famous British Association meeting in Oxford in 1860. Unfortunately for him he came up against Huxley, and was demolished. This *Vanity Fair* cartoon reminds one that he was nicknamed 'Soapy Sam'. *Thames and Hudson Archives*

'DARWIN'S BULLDOG'—T. H. Huxley, caricatured by 'Ape' of *Vanity Fair* in the series 'Men of the Day'. *Thames and Hudson Archives*

78 'HAVE YOU NO RESPECT for fine lawn sleeves?' Darwin wrote, with mock nervousness, to Huxley after the Oxford debate. 'By Jove, you seem to have done it well.' Cartoon by 'Ape' in *Vanity Fair* 'Men of the Day' series. *Thames and Hudson Archives*

79 ERNST HAECKEL (1834–1919), Darwin's most influential supporter in Germany, was Professor of Zoology at Jena, and a widely read scientific popularizer. *By courtesy of the National Library of Medicine, Washington*

80 'DAS KAPITAL', second edition, inscribed by the author to 'Mr Charles Darwin, on the part of his sincere admirer Karl Marx, London, 16 June 1873, 1 Modena Villas, Maitland Park'. *Down House*

81 COMMEMORATIVE MEDAL struck in Moscow in 1959 for the centenary of the publication of *The Origin*. Obverse: 'Charles Darwin 1809–1882'. Reverse: 'Origin of Species · 100 years · 1859–1959'. *By courtesy of Dr H. B. D. Kettlewell*

82 THE FIFTIETH ANNIVERSARY of the publication of *The Origin of Species* was celebrated at Cambridge in 1909, in a ceremony which was graced by the presence of Sir Joseph Hooker, Mrs T. H. Huxley (with a very young member of the Darwin family on her lap), and Lady Hooker. *By courtesy of Sir Julian Huxley*

83 AT CHICAGO, during the 1959 centennial, a Gilbert-and-Sullivan-style musical was performed. Here Huxley answers Bishop Wilberforce, singing
'I don't see that the Bishop has reason to sneer,
And I have no wish to abuse him;
But taking his line,
If I had to incline
Toward ape or divine,
Would I choose him?'
By courtesy of Professor Sol Tax

84-5 'SOME DOMESTIC RACES OF THE ROCK PIGEON differ fully as much from each other in external characters as do the most distinct natural genera' (*The Variation of Animals and Plants under Domestication*, Chapter 5). The rock pigeon, *Columba livia*, is a stuffed specimen; the pouter and carrier pigeons are drawings. *Down House*

86-7 THE DIFFERENT BREEDS of poultry, too, are the result of human selection. Fanciers ask, says Darwin, 'Can differences in climate, food and treatment have produced birds so different as the black stately Spanish, . . . and the Polish fowl with its great top-knot?' Drawings from *The Variation of Animals and Plants under Domestication*.

89 CARTOON, one of many on the same theme, from the *Hornet* of 22 March 1871. *Thames and Hudson Archives*

90 THE MALE ORANG-UTAN, Alexander, readily learnt to paint pictures. *Fox Photos*

91 'DARWIN'S POINT', occasionally occurring in both man and monkey, is a vestige, Darwin held, of their quadruped ancestry. Drawing from *The Descent of Man*

92 AUSTRALOPITHECUS—a reconstruction by Maurice Wilson. With astonishing acumen, Darwin suggested that the genus *Homo* had probably originated in Africa. *By courtesy of the Trustees, British Museum (Natural History)*

93 NORTHERN ELEPHANT SEAL (*Mirounga angustirostris*)—an example of the evolutionary advantage of great size and strength, when there is polygamy, and sexual selection is by physical combat. *By courtesy of R. Boolootian and G. A. Bartholomew, Department of Zoology, University of California, Los Angeles*

94 WEAPONS IN SEXUAL SELECTION. The enormous jaws and horns of some male beetles seem to have evolved by sexual selection as organs of threat as well as of combat. Drawings from *The Descent of Man*

95 MUTUAL DISPLAY IN BIRDS: the extraordinary 'penguin dance' display of the great crested grebe, serving as a bonding ritual for the pair. Painting by Gilbert Spencer, RA. *By courtesy of Sir Julian Huxley*

96 VOCAL DISPLAY: in the prairie chicken (*Tetrao cupido*), 'the male has two bare, orange-coloured sacks, one on each side of the neck; and these are largely inflated when the male, during the breeding-season, makes his curious hollow sound, audible at a great distance'. Drawing from *The Descent of Man*

97 STUDIO PORTRAIT in his late forties by Maull & Fox, *c.* 1856. *Thames and Hudson Archives*

99 THE MID-VICTORIAN BUSTLE: an example of how feminine fashions often exaggerate natural features which are sexually attractive. *Thames and Hudson Archives*

100 GIRAFFE-NECKED WOMAN OF BURMA: a sixteen-year-old girl, her neck elongated by eighteen inches of brass rings weighing 25 lb., provides a living example of artificial exaggeration of secondary sexual differences in man. *Black Star*

101 HORROR AND AGONY are counterfeited in the old man's expression by slight electric shocks delivered to the appropriate facial muscles. Illustration from *The Expression of the Emotions in Man and Animals*, copied from a photograph in Duchenne's *Mécanisme de la physionomie humaine*. Dr Duchenne gave Darwin much material for the illustration of his book.

102 'IT IS EASY TO OBSERVE INFANTS whilst screaming,' Darwin observed, not very grammatically; 'but I have found photographs made by the instantaneous process the best means for observation, as allowing more deliberation.' His interest in this subject dates from the birth of his first child, in 1839. Illustration from *The Expression of the Emotions in Man and Animals* (1872)

103 IN ANIMALS TOO Darwin watched the expression of the basic emotions, and studied their expression in terms of biologically meaningful behaviour. Illustration from *The Expression of the Emotions* . . .

104 HE DESCRIBED AN ANTITHESIS of attitude in antithetical emotions: in the hostile dog, tail and hair are erect, legs and body stiff; the affectionate dog's tail is down, its hair smooth, its whole attitude relaxed. 'This theory', he noted, 'has not met with much acceptance.' Today it is regarded as obvious. Illustration from *The Expression of the Emotions* . . .

105 IN THE BABOON, *Cynopithecus niger*, pleasure, as when being caressed, takes a strange form. 'The corners of the mouth are . . . drawn backwards and upwards, so that the teeth are exposed. Hence this expression would never be recognized by a stranger as one of pleasure.' Illustration from *The Expression of the Emotions* . . .

106 A DISPLACEMENT-ACTIVITY utilized in courtship. Ritualized preening forms a conspicuous part of male display in various ducks. (1) Shelduck, (2) Garganey, (3) Mandarin, (4) Mallard. From N. Tinbergen, *Social Behaviour in Animals* (after Lorenz). *By courtesy of the author and Messrs Methuen & Co. Ltd*

107 MALE ARGUS PHEASANT displaying. Another example of how the high premium on mating success in polygamous species brings about exaggerated development of male secondary sexual characters. Illustration from *The Descent of Man*

108 'NATURE'S SECRET REVEALED': title-page of C. K. Sprengel's book in which he described for the first time the role played by insects in plant fertilization

109 THE PYRAMIDAL ORCHID, with detail drawings to show the ingenious method by which pollination is ensured. Illustration from *The Various Contrivances by which British and Foreign Orchids are Fertilized*

110 OPHRYS SPHEGODES, a British orchid which puzzled Darwin by its lack of nectar. Only recently has it been established that it is fertilized by 'pseudo-copulation', that is to say the insect mistakes the flower for a female insect. Drawing by E. J. Bedford. *By courtesy of the Trustees, British Museum (Natural History)*

111 HEAD AND PROBOSCIS of *Acontia luctuosa*, with seven pairs of pollinia, or pollenmasses, attached to it. Darwin loved to demonstrate fertilization of orchids by pushing a needle into the nectary, and withdrawing the pollen-masses on their

sticky stalks; the stalks would bend within half a minute, so that when presented to another flower the pollen was in the right position to attach itself to the stigmas. 'I have shown this little experiment to several persons, and all have expressed their liveliest admiration at the perfection of the contrivance by which the orchid is fertilized.' Illustration from *The Various Contrivances* . . .

112 A FASCINATING EXAMPLE of adaptation: *Catasetum saccatum*, with its 'hair-trigger' method of ensuring insect pollination. Drawings from *The Various Contrivances* . . .

114 THE PRIMROSE (*Primula vulgaris*), a plant with two forms of flower. *Left*, pin-eyed (long style, short stamens); *right*, thrum-eyed (short style, long stamens). Darwin showed that this simple mechanism favours cross-fertilization; that there must be some advantage in cross-fertilization; and that the mechanism is an adaptation preserved by natural selection. Drawing from *Darwinism* by Alfred Russel Wallace

115 THE THREE FORMS of flower in *Lythrum*, with three different lengths of style. Dotted lines show the routes by which cross-pollination takes place. From *Different Forms of Flowers* . . .

116 THE VIRGINIA CREEPER (*Ampelopsis hederacea*)—a plant adapted for both climbing and adhesion. *A*, a growing tendril reaching out. *B*, older tendril which has developed adhesive disks to attach it to a wall. Drawing by Sir George Darwin from *The Movements and Habits of Climbing Plants*

117 ON THE VERANDA at Down House. *Thames and Hudson Archives*

118 YOUNG FLOWER STALK of the vine, showing a tendril (*B*) 'adapted to aid in carrying the future bunch of grapes' that

will develop from the flowers buds on *C*. Drawing by Sir George Darwin from *The Movements and Habits of Climbing Plants*

119 DARWIN'S WALKING-STICK and his armchair on the veranda. *Down House*

120–1 A SUNDEW LEAF (*Drosera rotundifolia*), with extended tentacles and with those of one side inflected over a bit of meat placed on the disk. Drawings from *Insectivorous Plants*

122 THE WORM STONE was set in the lawn, and Darwin measured the rate at which the action of earthworms caused it to sink—approximately $\frac{1}{4}$ inch per year. *Down House*

123 THE DRAWING-ROOM at Down House. On the piano Darwin placed a pot of earthworms, and found that they reacted to a deep bass note, probably because of the vibration, since they took no notice when he played a bassoon to them. *Down House*

124 FALLEN MONOLITHS at Stonehenge were in process of being buried by earthworms, as Darwin showed. Painting by Richard Tongue, 1838. *By courtesy of the Trustees, British Museum*

125 THE LAST PHOTOGRAPH of Darwin that was taken. Ill and tired, warned by a heart attack, he continued working to the end. *Radio Times Hulton Picture Library*

127 'MAN IS BUT A WORM'. A *Punch* cartoon links the worm, emerging from primeval ooze, with man, and with a sympathetic, even affectionate, representation of the sage of Down. *Thames and Hudson Archives*

128 WALLACE AND DARWIN side by side: the memorial tablets in Westminster Abbey, fittingly placed above the tomb of Sir Isaac Newton. *By courtesy of the Dean and Chapter of Westminster*

Numbers in italics refer to the illustrations

Acontia, 111
adaptation, 43–4, 54, 108*ff.*, *116*, *118*, *120–1*
adaptive niches, 54
Agassiz, Louis, 79
Ainsworth, W. F., 13
Audubon, J. J., 13
Australia, 46

Bahia, 21, 24, *25*, 47
Bahia Blanca, 28, 32
barnacles, 71–3
Basket, Fuegia, 23, 30, 31
Bell, Sir Charles, 102–3
Browne, Dr Crichton, 104
Buenos Aires, 28, 32, 33, 34
Butler, Dr Samuel, 10
Button, Jemmy, 23, 30, 31, 35

Cambridge, *14*, 15–17
Case, Rev. G., 8
Catasetum, 112, 113
cats, 85, 115
Chagas' disease, 6, 38–9, 66
Climbing Plants, 116, 118
Cocos Islands, 47
Coldstream, Dr John, 13
Concepción, 40–1
Cope, E. D., 81
Copiapó, 42
coral reefs, 43, 47, 51
Coryanthes, 111
Covington, Simms, 22, 49
cross-fertilization, 108*ff.*
Cuvier, Baron de, 76, 79

Darwin, Caroline (sister), 8, 40, 45
Darwin, Catherine (sister), *9*
Darwin, Emma (wife), *56*, *57*, 65, 66
Darwin, Erasmus (grandfather), 8, 12, 66
Darwin, Erasmus Alvey (brother), 8, 12, *13*, 14
Darwin, Francis (son), 62, 116, 120, 121
Darwin, Leonard (son), 62, *63*
Darwin, Robert Waring (father), 7, *9*, 12, 14, 15, 66

Darwin, Susannah (mother), 8, *9*, 12
Darwin, William (son), 62, 102
Darwinism, social, 81
Darwin Museum, Moscow, 80
Descent of Man, The, 88ff.
Different Forms of Flowers . . . , 114
displacement activities, 106
display, 94–6, 97–8, *99*, *100*, 107
dogs, 85, 103, *104*
Down House, 60–1, 63–4, *69*
Drosera, 120–1
Duchenne, Dr Guillaume, 105
Duncan, Dr Andrew, 12

Earle, Augustus, 22, 25
earthworms, 61, 64, 122*ff.*
Edinburgh University, 11–14
Effects of Cross- and Self-Fertilization . . . , 114
ethology, 90, 106, 108
Expression of the Emotions . . . , The, 101, 102, 103ff.

Falkland Islands, 32
Farrar, Canon, 126
Fisher, R. A., 88, 112
FitzRoy, Captain Robert, 18, *20*, 21–2

Galápagos Islands, 43–4
Geological Observations on South America, 51
Glen Roy, 6, 51, 66
Gosse, Philip, 74, 76
Gould, John, 50
Grant, Dr Robert E., 12–13

Haeckel, Ernst, 79
Henslow, Rev. J. S., 16, 17, 18, 19, 21, 49
Hooker, Sir Joseph, 52, 60, 68–70, 73, 74, 82, 108, 126
Humboldt, Alexander von, 17, 21, 23, 24, 50
Huxley, Thomas Henry, 60, 73, 74, 75, 77–9, 80, 88, 126

Insectivorous Plants, 120

Index   Jameson, Robert, 14

King, Philip Gidley, 22, 25
Kingsley, Charles, 74

Lamarck, Chevalier de, 79
Lowell, Robert, 126
Lubbock, Sir John, 74
Lyell, Sir Charles, 26, 29, 52, 53, 69–70, 74
Lythrum, 114, *115*

Maer, 14, 18, 49, 56, 57, 59, 122
Magellan, Straits of, 36, *37*, *42*
Maldonado, 32
Malthus, Thomas, 55
Marsh, Othniel, 81
Marx, Karl, 6, 80
Matthews, Rev. Richard, 30, 31
Mendel, Gregor, 85
Monro, Dr Alexander, 12
Montevideo, 27, 28–9
Müller, Fritz, 81
Musters, Charles, 22, 26
mutability of species, 44, 52
mutation, 85, 87

Newton, Alfred, 73, 74
New Zealand, 45

Ophrys, *110*, 111
orchids, 109–12
Orchis pyramidalis, *109*, 111
Origin of Species, The, 66, 70, 71, 73, 74, 76ff.
Owen, Sir Richard, 50, 76, 77–8

pangenesis, 87–8
pigeons, 84, *84–5*
platypus, 46
Port Desire, *34*, 35
Primula, 113, *114*
pseudo-copulation, 111

Raverat, Gwen, 60, 61, 65
Rio de Janeiro, 22, 25, 26, *27*

Rio Negro, 32, 35
Rio Santa Cruz, 36

Sachs, Julius von, 118
St Jago, 23
Sarmiento, Mount, 37
Sedgwick, Adam, 16, 17, 19, 48, 49, 76
selection, artificial, 54, 87
selection, natural, 73, 74, 88, 100, 108, 112
selection, sexual, 93ff.
Shrewsbury School, 10, *11*, 49
Spencer, Herbert, 74
Sprengel, C. K., 108
Stokes, John Lort, 22
Stonehenge, 124
Sullivan, Bartholomew James, 22

Tahiti, 45
Tenerife, 23
Thompson, Sir Harry, 16
Thompson, Vaughan, 72
Tierra del Fuego, 30, *31*, 35, 48
Time Will Tell, 82–3
Trimen, Henry, 77
Tristram, Canon, 74

Valparaiso, 37, 41, 42
variation, 83ff., *84*, 87
Variation of Animals and Plants . . . , The, 83ff.
Volcanic Islands, 51

Wallace, Alfred Russel, 6, *68*, 69–70, 73, 74, 81, 91, 126
Waterton, Charles, 13, 22
Way, Albert, 16
Wedgwood, Josiah (of Maer), 14, 18, 19, 56, 122
Whewell, Dr William, 16
White, Adam, 77
White, Gilbert, 10
Wilberforce, Bishop, 77–8
Worm Stone, 61, *122*

York Minster (Fuegian native), 23, 30, 31